آئینۂ قیامت

'A'ina e Qiyamat

A REFLECTION OF DOOMSDAY

'Ā'ina e Qiyāmat

A REFLECTION OF DOOMSDAY

THE MASSACRE OF KARBALA

'USTĀDH AL-ZAMAN

`Allāmah Ḥasan Riḍā' al-Baraylawī

TRANSLATION

Muftī Sayyid `Abdul Ṣamad al-Qādirī

TheSunniWay

A REFLECTION OF DOOMSDAY

contact@thesunniway.com

ISBN: 978-1-957773-10-0

DEDICATION

My grandfather-in-law,

\`ALLĀMAH SHĀH TURĀB AL-ḤAQ QĀDIRĪ

May Allāh have mercy upon him.

The grandson of the Noble Messenger, may Allāh send blessings and salutations upon him, who displayed exemplary loyalty to the path of 'A\`lā Ḥaḍrat, may Allāh have mercy upon him.

FAQĪR SAYYID \`ABDUL ṢAMAD AL-QĀDIRĪ

Khādim, TheSunniWay

CONTENTS

حسين رضي الله عنه

PREFACE BY THE GRANDSON OF SADR AL-SHARI`AH

ALLĀH'S NAME TO BEGIN WITH, THE MOST COMPASSIONATE, THE EVER-MERCIFUL.

'Ā'ina-e-Qiyāmat is the renowned book written by the brother of 'A`lā Ḥaḍrat, the expert of knowledge and literature, the Honorable `Allāmah Ḥasan Riḍā' Khān, upon him be mercy and divine pleasure, which has been written based upon the occurrences of *Karbalā*. The occurrence of *Karbalā* is a tragedy of 'Islāmic history which shall not be forgotten for as long as the world exists. This is a stain on 'Islāmic history; we feel ashamed at the mention of this occurrence before other nations. This question is in every heart and upon every tongue that: what and how has such an event transpired, that after fifty years of the passing of the Messenger of the Muslims, upon him be blessings and salutations, upon whom the Muslims are sacrificed by heart and soul, such circumstances came to life amongst them that amongst the same people who recite the *shahādah* of that very Prophet, some people made his family members the target of their swords? The intellect is astonished. The heart is in anguish. However, this is an occurrence which cannot be denied.

In the explicit passages of the *Qur'ān* & *Ḥadīth*, the virtues of the household of His Sanctified Eminence, may Allāh send blessings and salutations upon him, are displayed concerning which the entire nation is in consensus. Likewise, none can deny the tragedy of *Karbalā*, and there is no room for denying that Yazīd's political lust for leadership had complete interference in this. The caliphate of *Banū 'Umayyah* remained even after the occurrences of *Karbalā* for approximately eighty years, and their methodology persisted and spread throughout the 'Islāmic world. All narrators of the history of *Karbalā* are of the same era. These historical narratives were compiled at a later time. It is apparent that under such circumstances, it is unimaginable that there would be no alteration, omission, and fabrication [in the narrations]. Thus, if you study *al-Bidāyah wa al-Nihāyah* and various other books of history, you will find all sorts of narrations. If all of these narrations are compiled in one place, the entire event of *Karbalā* will be left as a riddle due to which some imbeciles denied the occurrence of *Karbalā*.

These same narrations were also made the basis for whichever book was written in this regard thereafter, and upon numerous occasions, no distinction was made between the moist and dry. To differentiate between moist and dry amongst historical narratives, some principles are required. However, the aim of historians is generally that in any fashion whatsoever, history be compiled – and that is all. Similar is the case for the majority of books written in Urdu. Thus, the reliable noble scholars tread with utmost caution in the mention of martyrdom lest any erroneous report be attributed to those People of the Household, may Allāh be pleased with them.

In this regard, the book *'Ā'ina-e-Qiyāmat* of the brother of 'A`lā Ḥaḍrat, the Honorable `Allamah Mawlānā Ḥasan Riḍā' Khān Baraylawī, is a considerable and reliable text as this book has come from the household of 'A`lā Ḥaḍrat, may his secret be sanctified, and 'A`lā Ḥaḍrat has also demonstrated reliance upon it.

By means of the reliance of the *'Imām* of the *'Ahl al-Sunnah*, this book has become a brilliant asset for us. If the readers observe the method of this book, [they will find] it is somewhat different from the books written [previously] based upon the mention of martyrdom; everything has been derived from reliable sources.

It is the good fortune of my very righteous student, Mawlānā Sayyid `Abdul Ṣamad Raḍawī, that he found the opportunity to work on this, and by translating this into English, he fulfilled this academic duty with diligence. I feel great contentment that Mawlānā Sayyid `Abdul Ṣamad Raḍawī is giving a reliable resource to the young orators of the western lands. The aforementioned has done a favor upon the English-speaking people by presenting this book in their language. May Allāh Almighty grant him the reward of this in this world and in the hereafter and grant this book widespread acceptance. *'Āmīn.*

FAQĪR FAIZĀN UL-MUṢṬAFĀ QĀDIRĪ

Jāmi`ah 'Imām-e-'A`ẓam 'Abū Ḥanīfah, Lucknow, India

Dhū al-Ḥijjah 15, 1444 Hijrī | July 3, 2023

TRANSLATOR'S NOTE

ALLĀH'S NAME TO BEGIN WITH, THE MOST COMPASSIONATE, THE EVER-MERCIFUL.

By the *tawfīq* granted by Allāh Almighty, the translation of *'Ā'ina-e-Qiyāmat* has been completed, and by the will of Allāh Almighty, this work will play a significant role in the English-speaking audiences learning about the heartbreaking massacre of *Karbalā*.

It has become all too common for speakers and writers to loosen their grip on moderation when mentioning this occurrence, and it is seen that many purposely resort to the narrations of the misguided when seeking a flow of tears from the eyes of the audience.

In modern times, the audacious, when criticizing the malicious Yazīd, fall into extremes and extend their gaze to a zone wherein the believer's tongue will not utter but good.

They maliciously extend their criticisms to the court of the noble Companion, Sayyidunā 'Amīr Mu`āwiyah, may Allāh be pleased with him, for the doings of his malicious son due to his appointment of him as his succeeding ruler.

However, even this criticism, when put under the lens of justice, fails to prevail as it is narrated that during a sermon, Sayyidunā 'Amīr Mu`āwiyah, may Allāh be pleased with him, beseeched Allāh Almighty saying:

اللهم إن كنت إنما عهدت ليزيد لما رأيت من فضله فبلغه ما أملت وأعنه وإن كنت إنما
حملني حب الوالد لولده وأنه ليس لما صنعت به أهلا فاقبضه قبل أن يبلغ ذلك

"O Allāh, if I have granted authority to Yazīd only due to what I see of his merit, then allow him to reach what I have hoped and aid him. And if merely the love of a father for his seed has influenced me, and he is not worthy of what I have arranged for him, then take him away before he reaches that." [1]

Sayyidunā 'Amīr Mu`āwiyah, may Allāh be pleased with him, is publicly beseeching Allāh Almighty to take the life of his own son if he is not worthy of the position for which he himself has deemed fit.

What was apparent to Sayyidunā 'Amīr Mu`āwiyah, may Allāh be pleased with him, was that Yazīd was an individual worthy of such a position and nothing that he saw in him at the time implied the contrary.

The sincerity in the heart of Sayyidunā 'Amīr Mu`āwiyah, may Allāh be pleased with him, for the Muslim nation led him to ask Allāh Almighty for that which a sincere father would never ask for his son, and yet the wicked seek to carry the blame of *Karbalā* to his virtuous court.

Moreover, on the other end of the extreme, there are people shameless enough to refer to the massacre of *Karbalā* as a "battle of two princes" showing reverence to Yazīd due to his relation to his noble father.

These are the words of an individual who bears not an ounce of shame, and nor is such thinking the way of the pious predecessors.

[1] *Tārīkh al-Khulafā', Yazīd bin Mu`āwiyah 'Abū Khālid al-'Umawī*

The teaching of the *Salaf* in this regard is simply that Yazīd was a filthy son of a noble father; the horrendous acts of Yazīd do not harm the status of Sayyidunā 'Amīr Mu`āwiyah, may Allāh be pleased with him, and the lofty rank of Sayyidunā 'Amīr Mu`āwiyah, may Allāh be pleased with him, was not inherited by the filthy Yazīd. This is the teaching of the *Salaf*. In the court of Sayyidunā `Umar bin `Abd al-`Azīz, may Allāh be pleased with him, a man insulted Sayyidunā 'Amīr Mu`āwiyah, may Allāh be pleased with him, and the Noble Khalīfah flogged him because of it. Another man said, "'Amīr al-Mu'minīn Yazīd" and Sayyidunā `Umar bin `Abd al-`Azīz, may Allāh be pleased with him, flogged him as well.[2] This is the moderation of the pious predecessors in this regard, and this is a model which is to be followed by the Muslims.

Unfortunately, such moderation is not common, and this widespread epidemic of both extremes has caused it to become more difficult for the masses to learn of the sacrifices made by the Noble Household of Sayyidunā Rasūl Allāh, may Allāh send blessings and salutations upon him, in protecting the glorious religion of *'Islām* and to learn the details of the atrocities that took place against them in the battlefield of *Karbalā*.

The Noble Sayyidunā 'Imām 'Aḥmad Riḍā', may Allāh have mercy upon him, was asked about listening to the events of *Karbalā* and he responded, "Authentic narrations are either in the book of Shāh `Abd al-`Azīz Ṣāḥib which is in Arabic or my late brother Ḥasan Miyāñ's book, *'Ā'inā e Qiyāmat*, and they should be

[2] *al-Nibrās, Nakuffu `an Dhikr al-Ṣaḥābah 'illā bi Khayr*

listened to. Moreover, not reading and not listening is better than reading erroneous reports." [3]

This is a work upon which 'A`lā Ḥadrat, may Allāh have mercy upon him, himself has placed his seal of approval, thus making this work one which conveys the message and story of *Karbalā* in a manner which is in accordance with the teachings of the pious predecessors and the reliable scholars of the past; this is a text which explains these incidents without transgressing the parameters of moderation.

I ask Allāh Almighty to make this attempted translation as beneficial as the original work, and I ask Allāh Almighty to reward all those involved in this project abundantly. *Faqīr* was only an insignificant piece in the completion of this work, and I extend my appreciation to the people whose valuable efforts made it possible for this effort to reach the reader: Muftī Faizān ul-Muṣṭafā Qādirī, Muftī Zāhid Ḥussain al-Qādirī, Muftī Sayyid 'Asad al-Qādirī, Muftī Salmān al-Nūrī, Muftī Sohel al-Qādirī, and many others who gave their time in proofreading the translation. May Allāh Almighty protect them all and continue to allow the *'Ahl al-Sunnah* to benefit from their efforts.

FAQĪR `ABDUL ṢAMAD AL-QĀDIRĪ

Servant of the Dīn at TheSunniWay USA

Dhū al-Ḥijjah 10, 1444 Hijrī | June 28, 2023

[3] *al-Malfūẓ, Vol. 2, Pg. 293*

ALLĀH'S NAME TO BEGIN WITH, THE MOST COMPASSIONATE, THE EVER-MERCIFUL.

All praise is for Allāh, the Lord of all Worlds, and may blessings and salutations be upon our master and chief, Muḥammad, and all his progeny and companions.

I

THE PRESENCE OF THE VIRTUE OF MARTYRDOM IN THE COURT OF ALLAH'S BELOVED ﷺ

Allāh Almighty has made Our Luminous Eminence, the Master of the Universe, may Allāh Almighty send blessings and salutations upon him and his progeny, the incarnate of all perfections and qualities. The praiseworthy qualities and cherished characteristics akin to that of His Eminence, may Allāh Almighty send blessings and salutations upon him and his progeny, are not possible in any Angel, human, Messenger, or Prophet.

Upon first glance, it is the virtue of martyrdom alone which was deprived of a visit in his `*Arsh*-imitant court.

Regarding this, the opinion of the noble `*ulamā'* is – and what a refined opinion it is – that in the battle of *'Uḥud Sharīf*, the wounding of the blessed teeth of that Imaged Soul and Embodiment of Life, may Allāh Almighty send blessings and salutations upon him and his progeny, is superior to the martyrdom of every martyr.

Furthermore, when the mind reflects on the heartfelt bond of His Luminous Eminence, may Allāh Almighty send blessings and salutations upon him and his progeny, with the princes, there remains no hesitation in the fact manifesting that the martyrdom of these honorable individuals is the martyrdom of His Eminence, may Allāh Almighty send blessings and salutations upon him and his progeny, himself. They granted prosperity and esteem to this honor in his representation.

2

THE VIRTUES OF 'IMAM HASAN AND 'IMAM HUSAYN

Sayyidunā 'Imām Ḥasan, Allāh Almighty is pleased with him, once presented himself in the august court and ascended the blessed shoulder of His Luminous Eminence, may Allāh Almighty send blessings and salutations upon him and his progeny. A companion commented, "O prince, how wonderful is your carrier." His Sanctified Eminence, may Allāh send blessings and salutations upon him and his progeny, responded, "And how wonderful of a passenger is the passenger." [4]

His Luminous Eminence, may Allāh Almighty send blessings and salutations upon him and his progeny, was in *sajdah* when

[4] *Sunan al-Tirmidhī, Kitāb al-Manāqib, Bāb Manāqib 'Abū Muḥammad al-Ḥasan, Ḥadīth: 3809, Vol. 5, Pg. 432*

'Imām Ḥasan, Allāh Almighty is pleased with him, embraced his blessed back.

His Eminence, upon him be blessing and salutation, prolonged the *sajdah* lest he falls upon raising the head.[5]

It is stated regarding 'Imām Ḥasan and 'Imām Ḥusayn, Allāh Almighty is pleased with them both, "These two sons of ours are the leaders of the youth in Paradise." [6] Furthermore, it is stated, "Their ally is our ally. Their enemy is our enemy." [7]

Moreover, he states, "These two are the swords of the *`Arsh*." He also says, "Ḥusayn is from me, and I am from Ḥusayn. May Allāh befriend whomsoever befriends Ḥusayn. Ḥusayn is a grandson from amongst the grandsons." [8]

One day, seated on the right thigh of His Luminous Eminence, may Allāh Almighty send blessings and salutations upon him and his progeny, was 'Imām Ḥusayn, may Allāh be pleased with him, and on the left was the prince of His Eminence, may Allāh Almighty send blessings and salutations upon him and his progeny, Sayyidunā 'Ibrāhīm, Allāh Almighty is pleased with him.

[5] *Musnad 'Abū Ya`lā, Musnad 'Anas bin Mālik, Ḥadīth: 3415, Vol. 3, Pg. 21*

[6] *Sunan al-Tirmidhī, Kitāb al-Manāqib, Bāb Manāqib 'Abū Muḥammad al-Ḥasan, Ḥadīth: 3793, Vol. 5, Pg. 426*

[7] *Sunan 'Ibn Mājah, Kitāb al-Sunnah, Bāb Faḍl al-Ḥasan wa al-Ḥusayn, Ḥadīth: 143, Vol. 1, Pg. 96*

[8] *Sunan al-Tirmidhī, Kitāb al-Manāqib, Bāb Manāqib 'Abū Muḥammad al-Ḥasan, Ḥadīth: 3800, Vol. 5, Pg. 429*

Sayyidunā Jibrīl, upon him be salutations, presented himself and humbly requested, "Allāh will not keep both of them with His Eminence, may Allāh Almighty send blessings and salutations upon him and his progeny. Please select one."

His Eminence, may Allāh Almighty send blessings and salutations upon him and his progeny, did not tolerate the separation of 'Imām Ḥusayn, Allāh Almighty is pleased with him, and three days later, Sayyidunā 'Ibrāhīm, Allāh Almighty is pleased with him, passed away. Following this occurrence, when he would present himself, he, may Allāh Almighty send blessings and salutations upon him and his progeny, would kiss him and say:

مرحبا بمن فديته بابنی

Welcome to the one I redeemed with my own son.[9]

He also used to say, "These two are my sons and the sons of my daughter. O Allāh, I befriend them, You too befriend them and befriend whoever befriends them!"[10] He used to say to Batūl Zahrā,[11] Allāh Almighty is pleased with her, "Bring both of my sons." He would then smell them and embrace them to the illuminated chest.[12]

[9] *Tārīkh Baghdād, Vol. 2, Pg. 200, Bi Lafẓ: "Fadaytu Man"*

[10] *Sunan al-Tirmidhī, Kitāb al-Manāqib, Bāb Manāqib 'Abū Muḥammad al-Ḥasan, Ḥadīth: 3794, Vol. 5, Pg. 427*

[11] *This is a title of Sayyidah Fāṭimah, Allāh is pleased with her, which translates to "The Pure Rose." (Translator)*

[12] *Sunan al-Tirmidhī, Kitāb al-Manāqib, Bāb Manāqib 'Abū Muḥammad al-Ḥasan, Ḥadīth: 3797, Vol. 5, Pg. 428*

3

THE BELOVEDS OF ALLAH AND HIS CUSTOM

When the words of His Luminous Eminence, may Allāh Almighty send blessings and salutations upon him and his progeny, and such consolations and commendations of the princes come to mind, and the gaze falls to the episodes of martyrdom, the eyes of astonishment do not shed tears, but drops of blood.

The world of Allāh's Almighty sovereignty captures the vision.

These sanctified figures are friends to Allāh Almighty, and it is the noble custom of Allāh, majestic is His majesty, that He besieges His friends with hardships in the worldly life.

One companion said, "I possess love for His Eminence."

He responded, "Prepare for poverty."

He stated, "I take Allāh Almighty as a friend."

He replied, "Brace yourself for hardship."

He also states, "The most severe hardship befalls the Prophets, upon them be blessing and commendation. Then, those who are best. Then, those who are best."[13]

نزدیکاں را بیش بود حیرانی

The close ones are astonished more.

جن کے رتبے ہیں سوا ان کو سوا مشکل ہے

Those of colossal status receive colossal hardship.

[13] *al-Musnad li al-'Imām 'Aḥmad, Ḥadīth. 27147, Vol. 10, Pg. 306*

4

THE VOLUNTARY MODESTY OF THE MASTER AND HIS NOBLE HOUSEHOLD

May Allāh Almighty Send Blessings and Salutations Upon Him and His Progeny

Allāh Almighty made Our Eminence, may Allāh Almighty send blessings and salutations upon him and his progeny, the superior-most creation and granted him the glorious robe of exclusive affection.

For this reason, it is not possible for any other to bear the trials of the world that he, may Allāh Almighty send blessings and salutations upon him and his progeny, faced and the difficulties that he, may Allāh Almighty send blessings and salutations upon him and his progeny, endured. Allāh, Allāh!

The manifestations of love are such that it is said:

لولاك لما خلقت الدنيا

O beloved, had I not created you,

I would not have created the world.[14]

Such modes of elevating rank, that He granted you the keys to His treasures, making you the absolute authority so you may do as you please. You have the jurisdiction of black and white.

He is such a king on whose sanctified head the glistening crown of rule on both worlds has been placed. He is so eminent that the throne of Allāh has been spread beneath his blessed feet. The world's rulers are in need of his royal distribution. The great kings are dependent on his imperial charity. The distributor of the world's bounties, the grantor of the era's riches fills the laps of the beggars and fulfills whatever wishes are expressed. When the gaze now turns to the sanctified abode and the sacred residence, the grandeur of Allāh Almighty is evident. He is a king of such majestic stature that his subduing rule has encompassed the east and west, and he is renowned throughout the seven skies and the entire face of the earth.

However, in his chosen home, there is not a thing of luxury. Never mind modes of comfort, he did not even eat dry dates or bread of unfiltered barley flour to a full stomach his entire life.

[14] *Firdaws al-'Akhbār, Ḥadīth: 8095, Vol. 2, Pg. 458, Bi Lafẓ: Mā Khalaqtu*

کل جہاں ملک اور جو کی روٹی غذا
اس شکم کی قناعت پہ لاکھوں سلام

The entire universe in possession, and bread of barley for nourishment
Thousands of salutations be upon the contentment of that abdomen[15]

Look at the royal attire to see seventeen patches – those too not from a single cloth. For two months at a time, smoke does not rise from the royal kitchen. This is the state of worldly comfort and luxury.

If you look at his religious prestige, then both worlds echo the splendor of that mantled king, may Allāh Almighty send blessings and salutations upon him and his progeny, and the grandeur of that ascetic.

مالک کونین ہیں گو پاس کچھ رکھتے نہیں
دو جہاں کی نعمتیں ہیں ان کے خالی ہاتھ میں

He owns both realms yet keeps nothing with himself
The bounties of both worlds are in his empty hands[16]

The matter worthy of noting here is that these difficulties and afflictions were taken on solely by his own pleasure; there was absolutely no compulsion in this.

Once, his Well-Wishing and Pleasure-Seeking Friend, majestic is His majesty, sent a message to him. He said, "If you say, We will make two mountains of *Makkah* (called *'Akhshabayn*) gold so that they remain with you."

[15] *Ḥadā'iq e Bakhshish*

[16] *ibid*

He responded, "I want that one day You give, so that I be grateful, and one day allow me to starve, so that I be patient." [17]

O Muslims! Allāh Almighty has bestowed unto Our Eminence, upon him be blessings and salutations, a content soul. Had he lived in lavish and luxury and gave preference to amenity and relaxation, his, may Allāh Almighty send blessings and salutations upon him and his progeny, Lord, the One pleased by his pleasure, would have sent many a Paradise onto land, and these modes of comfort would surely not have caused any change in his, may Allāh Almighty send blessings and salutations upon him and his progeny, chosen and pure soul. Favoring trial and befriending affliction in such a case can only be based on him being the Mercy to all the Worlds. He came as a mercy in favor of everything of this world. Had he, may Allāh Almighty send blessings and salutations upon him and his progeny, remained engaged in comfort and relaxation, then hardship and affliction, which will not even accompany the slaves of His Eminence, upon him be blessings and salutations, in the hereafter, would have become deprived of blessings.

Once, His Eminence, may Allāh Almighty send blessings and salutations upon him and his progeny, was distributing servants and bondswomen to the Muslims. Mawlā `Alī, may Allāh Almighty ennoble his countenance, said to Lady Batūl Zahrā, Allāh Almighty is pleased with her, "Go, you too bring yourself a bondswoman."

[17] *Sunan al-Tirmidhī, Kitāb al-Zuhd, Bāb Mā Jā'a fī al-Kifāf, Vol. 4, Pg. 155, Ḥadīth: 2354*

She presented herself and showed her hand while saying, "I have blisters on my hands resulting from grinding the mill. Grant me one bondswoman as well!"

It was said, "O Fāṭimah, I will inform you of something that will be of more benefit than a bondswoman or servant. While going to sleep at night, recite '*Subḥān Allāh*' thirty-three times, '*al-Ḥamdu li Allāh*' thirty-three times, and '*Allāhu 'Akbar*' thirty-four times preceding sleep." [18]

Once, His Luminous Eminence, may Allāh Almighty send blessings and salutations upon him and his progeny, entered the abode of Lady Fāṭimah, Allāh Almighty is pleased with her. He had just appeared at the door when he saw a bangle of silver in the hand of Fāṭimah, Allāh Almighty is pleased with her, and he retreated. Lady Batūl, Allāh Almighty is pleased with her, presented those bangles so that they may be given as charity, and were thus granted to the destitute people and two bangles of ivory were granted [to her]. It was said, "Fāṭimah, the world is not worthy of Muḥammad, nor the family of Muḥammad." May Allāh Almighty send blessings and salutations upon him and upon them.

`Umar al-Fārūq, Allāh Almighty is pleased with him, presented himself and saw that he is resting on a mat of date leaves. Marks from the mat had formed on that delicate physique and graceful body.

[18] *Sunan al-Tirmidhī, Kitāb al-Da`wāt, Bāb Mā Jā'a fī al-Tasbīḥ, Ḥadīth: 3419, Vol. 5, Pg. 260*

Upon seeing such a state, he began crying uncontrollably and said, "O Messenger of Allāh, Caesar and Khosrow, enemies of Allāh, live in pride and bounty, and the Beloved of Allāh in hardship and affliction?!"

It was stated, "Are you not pleased with the fact that they received the comfort of the world and that you are destined for the bounties of the afterlife?" [19]

[19] *Ṣaḥīḥ al-Bukhārī, Kitāb al-Tafsīr, Bāb Tabtaghī Marḍāt, Ḥadīth: 4913, Vol. 3, Pg. 360*

THE TRUE FRIENDS OF ALLAH ALMIGHTY

By means of divine inspiration (*'ilhām*), Sayyidunā Sirrī al-Saqaṭī, may Allāh Almighty have mercy upon him, was told, "O Sirrī, I made the creation and asked it, 'Do you befriend Me?' Unanimously, everyone responded, 'Who is there besides You we would befriend?' Then I created the world, and nine tenths went towards it. One tenth said, 'We will not disassociate from You for its sake.' Then, I created the afterlife and nine tenths of that one tenth became its consumers. The remainder said, 'We neither ask for the world, and nor are we inclined towards the hereafter. We are those who yearn for You.' Thereafter, afflictions were inflicted and even from them, nine tenths were startled and became distressed. The remaining one tenth said, 'If You turn the fourteen levels of land and sky into a leash of affliction and place it on our necks, we will still not turn on You.'"

Regarding them, it was said:

أولئك أوليائي حقا

They are My friends in reality.

Now, the preference of affliction by the Noble *'Ahl al-Bayt,* Allāh Almighty is pleased with them, is worthy of being seen with the eyes of astonishment.

Sayyidunā 'Abū Dharr, Allāh Almighty is pleased with him, was asked about affliction and bounty. He said, "According to us, both are equal."

انچه از دوست می رسد نیکوست

Whatever comes from the friend is good.

When 'Imām Ḥasan, Allāh Almighty is pleased with him, learned of this, he said, "May Allāh have mercy on 'Abū Dharr, Allāh Almighty is pleased with him, but according to us *'Ahl al-Bayt,* affliction is superior to bounty as bounty also carries pleasure to the soul, whereas affliction is solely the pleasure of the Friend."

اللهم صل على سيدنا ومولانا محمد وعلى آله وأصحابه أجمعين

O Allāh send blessings upon our master and chief, Muḥammad, and upon all of his offspring and companions.

6

FILTHY YAZID TAKING THE THRONE AND PREPARATION FOR DOOMSDAY

The sixtieth year of *Hijrah* and the month of *Rajab* brought such heartbreaking luggage, the spectacle of which drags the eyes of the 'Islāmic world towards it forcibly, wherein gut-wrenching afflictions and unsettling hardships have gathered the means of helplessness and bewilderment to rattle faithful hearts and disturb Allāh-worshiping dispositions.

The filthy Yazīd soiling the throne of sultanate with his impure foot was the prelude to such unbearable atrocities whose mention forces the liver to be pushed up to the mouth and the heart to stagger in the chest with an unusual anxiety.

That outcast thought that the fortification of his rule and the increasing of his own disgraced honor relied solely on dyeing his impure sword with the sanctified and innocent blood of the Noble *'Ahl al-Bayt*.

With the corruption of this infernal being's intention, the winds of the era inverted, and poisonous blows came due to the pure chest of the evergreen blossoms being torn in the sorrow of perpetual flowers and newly bloomed roses. The garb of the delicate flowers from the green, prolific, and swaying garden of Muṣṭafā, may Allāh Almighty send blessings and salutations upon him and his progeny, was soiled as they wilted.

7

‘IMAM HASAN’S MARTYRDOM AND ADVICE TO HIS BROTHER

رضي الله عنه

The first attack of that scum was against Sayyidunā ‘Imām Ḥasan. He misled Ja`dah, the wife of the Lofty-Stationed ‘Imām (Sayyidunā ‘Imām Ḥasan), saying, “If you were to assassinate the ‘Imām by poisoning him, I would marry you.”

That ill-fated woman, in lust of becoming the queen consort, forsaking the companionship of the princes of Paradise and relinquishing the crown of the hereafter, embarked on the path of Hell. Several times, she gave him poison and it had no effect. Thereafter, she wholeheartedly filled her insides with coal of the hellfire and gave intensely severe poison to the Heaven-Bound ‘Imām, such that the intestines of this part of Muṣṭafā’s, may Allāh Almighty send blessings and salutations upon him and his progeny, soul spewed after being shred to pieces.

Upon hearing such distressing news, 'Imām Ḥusayn, Allāh Almighty is pleased with him, presented himself to his beloved brother. He sat near the head and said, "Who poisoned to His Eminence?"

He responded, "If it is who I think it is, then Allāh is a great avenger. If not, I seek not any penalty from the innocent."[20]

It is in one narration that he said, "Brother! People expect from us that we benefit them by interceding for them on the Day of Resurrection, not that we bring wrath and revenge into play with them."

واہ رے حلم کہ اپنا تو جگر ٹکڑے ہو | پھر بھی ایذائے ستم گر کے روا دار نہیں

So fascinating is forbearance that our soul be torn
Yet, another wrong of the oppressor as he remains inconsiderate

Then, the departing 'Imām, Allāh Almighty is pleased with him, bequeathed the arriving 'Imām, Allāh Almighty is pleased with him, saying, "Look Ḥusayn, remain vigilant of the fools of *Kūfah* lest they surround you in their talks and invite you, then abandon you when the time comes. Then, you will regret it and the time of rescue will have slipped away."

Undoubtedly, this bequest of the Lofty-Stationed 'Imām, Allāh Almighty is pleased with him, was worthy of being weighed in pearls and etched upon the heart. However, who can prevent the forthcoming event which destiny had made renowned much time ago?

[20] *Ḥilyah al-'Awliyā', al-Ḥasan bin `Alī, Ḥadīth: 1438, Vol. 2, Pg. 47 (Summarized)*

8

‘IMAM HUSAYN’S MARTYRDOM BEING FAMED EVEN PRIOR TO THE OCCURRENCE

رضي الله عنه

Three hundred years preceding the blessed arrival of His Eminence, the Master of the Universe, may Allāh Almighty send blessings and salutations upon him and his progeny, this poetic stanza was found written on a rock:

أترجو أمة قتلت حسينا   شفاعة جده يوم الحساب

Does the nation who assassinated Ḥusayn expect
The intercession of his grandfather, may Allāh Almighty send blessings and salutations upon him and his progeny, on the Day of Recompense?

This exact stanza was discovered written in a church of Roman lands and the writer was unidentified. It is mentioned in several narrations that His Eminence, the Master of the

Universe, may Allāh Almighty send blessings and salutations upon him and his progeny, was present in the home of the Mother of Believers, Lady 'Umm Salamah, Allāh Almighty is pleased with her. An angel who had never visited prior, received permission to visit from Allāh, blessed and exalted is He, and lovingly approached the court. His Luminous Eminence, may Allāh Almighty send blessings and salutations upon him and progeny, said to the Mother of Believers, Allāh Almighty is pleased with her, "Keep watch at the door, no one should enter."

Just as this happened, 'Imām Ḥusayn, Allāh Almighty is pleased with him, opened the door presenting himself in the court and leaped to sit in the lap of His Luminous Eminence, may Allāh Almighty send blessings and salutations upon him and his progeny. His Eminence, may Allāh Almighty send blessings and salutations upon him and his progeny, began expressing his love and the angel humbly asked, "Does His Eminence love him?"

He responded, "Yes."

He said, "The time is near wherein the followers of His Eminence will assassinate him. If His Eminence wills, I can show that land wherein he will be given the status of martyrdom."

Then he presented red soil, and according to one narration, sand, and according to another, pebbles. His Eminence, upon him be blessings and salutations, smelled it and said:

ریحِ کرب وبلاء

"The odor of distress and affliction."

This soil was then granted to the Mother of Believers, Allāh Almighty is pleased with her, and was told, "When this turns to blood, know that Ḥusayn has been martyred."

She kept that soil in a vial. The Mother of Believers, Allāh Almighty is pleased with her, says, "I used to say, 'What a harsh day it would be when this soil turns to blood.'" [21]

En route to *Ṣiffīn*, the Commander of the Faithful, Mawlā `Alī, may Allāh Almighty ennoble his countenance, passed by the land of *Karbalā*. He asked its name and the people responded, "*Karbalā*!"

He cried so much that the ground had become moist as a result of the tears.

He then stated, "I presented myself in the sanctified court of His Eminence, the Master of the Universe, may Allāh Almighty send blessings and salutations upon him and his progeny, and found him to be crying. I asked him the reason and he said, 'Jibrīl has just gone saying that my son Ḥusayn will be assassinated by the banks of the Euphrates in *Karbalā*. Then, Jibrīl gave me the soil of that place to smell. I could not bear it and thus the eyes began shedding tears.'"

It is in one narration, Mawlā `Alī, Allāh Almighty is pleased with him, passed by the location where the blessed grave of the Oppressed 'Imām is now.

He said, "Here their transportation will be made to sit, their saddles will be placed here, and here their blood shall fall. Some youth from the offspring, Allāh Almighty is pleased with them, of

[21] *al-Mu`jam al-Kabīr, Ḥadīth: 2817, 2818, 2819, Vol. 3, Pg. 108*

Muḥammad, may Allāh Almighty send blessings and salutations upon him, will be martyred in this battlefield for whom the land and sky will weep." [22]

اللهم صل على سيدنا محمد وعلى آله وأصحابه أجمعين

O Allāh send blessings upon our master, Muḥammad,
and upon all of his offspring and companions.

[22] *Dalā'il al-Nabuwwah li 'Abū Nu`aym al-'Isbahānī, Vol. 2, Pg. 147*

9

MADINAH SLIPS FROM THE OPPRESSED ‘IMAM

رضي الله عنه

When the filthy Yazīd had pleased his miserable heart with the assassination of ‘Imām Ḥasan, Allāh Almighty is pleased with him, this scoundrel thought of ‘Imām Ḥusayn, Allāh Almighty is pleased with him. He wrote a letter to Walīd, the governor of *Madīnah*:

“Demand the pledge of allegiance from Ḥusayn, `Abd Allāh ‘ibn `Umar, and `Abd Allāh ‘ibn Zubayr [Allāh Almighty is pleased with them], and do not grant any respite. ‘Ibn `Umar is a man who sits in the *masjid*, and ‘Ibn Zubayr will remain silent until he sees his chance. However, to take the pledge of allegiance from Ḥusayn [Allāh Almighty is pleased with him] is of utmost importance because this lion, the son of a lion, will not wait for an opportunity.”

Upon reading the letter, the governor sent a courier. The 'Imām responded, "Okay, we are coming."

He then said to `Abd Allāh 'ibn Zubayr, "This is no time for court. This invitation at an irregular time shows that the ruler has passed. This is why we are being summoned, so that the pledge of allegiance to Yazīd can be taken from us before the news spreads."

'Ibn Zubayr responded, "I feel the same way. What is your view in such a situation?" He said, "I will gather my youth and go. I will position my companions at the entrance before proceeding towards him." 'Ibn Zubayr replied, "I am suspicious of him." He ('Imām Ḥusayn) said, "He cannot do anything to me."

Thereafter, he went along with his companions. He advised the companions, "Once I summon you or you hear my voice rising, come inside, and until I return, do not move from here."

He said this and went inside. He found Marwān sitting by Walīd. He delivered *salām* and sat down. Walīd read the letter aloud and the contents were found to be exactly what had come to the blessed thoughts of His Eminence. Upon hearing the state of pledging allegiance, he said, "People like me do not hide and pledge allegiance. Gather everyone, take the pledge of allegiance, and then tell me."

Giving preference to safety, Walīd said, "That is fine! You be on your way." Marwān said, "If you leave him now and do not take the pledge of allegiance, such an opportunity will not come to hand until the blood of many lives is not shed. Stop him now. If he pledges allegiance, good. Otherwise, decapitate him."

Hearing this, the 'Imām, Allāh Almighty is pleased with him, stated, "'Ibn al-Zarqā'! Can you or he kill me? By Allāh! You have lied and have spoken mischievously!" He said this and returned. Marwān said to Walīd, "By Allāh! Such an opportunity will not arise again!"

Walīd said, "I do not prefer that I assassinate Ḥusayn, Allāh Almighty is pleased with him, for not pledging allegiance. I do not accept the assassination of Ḥusayn, Allāh Almighty is pleased with him, even in exchange for the entire world's property and prosperity. According to me, the one brought to account for the blood of Ḥusayn is insignificant in the court of the Subduing Lord." Marwān hypocritically said, "You are right." [23]

The man came again. He told him, "Let morning come," and he decided that in the night, a journey will be undertaken with the family intending [travel to] *Makkah*.

The 'Imām, Allāh Almighty is pleased with him, spent this night in the enlightened shrine of his Noble Grandfather, may Allāh Almighty send blessings and salutations upon him, as after all, separation awaits. He should at least embrace the sanctified lap of his Noble Grandfather, may Allāh Almighty send blessings and salutations upon him and his progeny, as he leaves, then Allāh knows whether this time will come about in life or not.

The 'Imām was in a slumber as he saw a dream. His Luminous Eminence, may Allāh Almighty send blessings and salutations upon him and his progeny, has honored him by his arrival, embraced him, and said, "Ḥusayn, the time approaches wherein

[23] *al-Kāmil fī al-Tārīkh, Dhikr Bay`ah Yazīd, Vol. 3, Pg. 377 (Summarized)*

you will be martyred in a state of thirst, and the martyrs have great ranks in Paradise."

His eyes opened upon seeing this. He got up and presented himself at the sanctified mausoleum for departure.

O Muslims! In the worldly life, this visit was the final visit of the 'Imām.

After presenting benedictions and salutations, he stood lowering his head. The sorrow of departure was pinching at the heart. Tears were continuously flowing from the eyes. The passion of sentiment birthed a tremble in the body. Anxieties have brought about a catastrophe. The heart says, "The head can go, but the feet should not move from here," and the need of when the morning comes knocking is that you leave soon.

He takes two steps then turns back again. Attachment to home twirls at the feet, "Where are you going?"

Necessity tugs at the clothing, "Why do you make delay?"

Inclination desires that he does not leave all his life, whereas pressures demand that he not delay a single moment.

Three quarters of the night on the fourth of *Sha`bān* had passed. The gentle breezes of the final part pats the sleepers to a slumber. Little by little, some whiteness has manifested within the golden color of the stars. The darkness of the black night seeks to gather its kilt. The entire city is tranquil. Neither the sound of anyone speaking reaches the ear, nor can the tread of any walker be heard. The doors of the entire city are shut. However, the awakenings occur at this very time in the homes of the Prophetic Household and the provisions for travel are being prepared. The items of necessity have been taken out.

The animals for transportation are readily standing at the doors. The loads have been tied. The veil has been prepared.

Here, the 'Imām's son, brother, nephew, and family members are ascending the animals. Elsewhere, the 'Imām, Allāh Almighty is pleased with him, exits from *Masjid Nabawī*. The *miḥrābs* have bowed in greeting. The minarets stand showing respect.

The caravan of the Prophet's offspring departs with the arrival of the caravanner.

Of the *'Ahl al-Bayt*, Allāh Almighty is pleased with them, only Lady Ṣughrā, the daughter of the Oppressed 'Imām, and the Noble Muḥammad bin Ḥanafīyyah, the son of Mawlā `Alī, Allāh Almighty is pleased with him, remain in *Madīnah*.

Allāhu 'Akbar! There was once a day wherein His Eminence, the Master of the Universe, may Allāh Almighty send blessings and salutations upon him and his progeny, migrated from *Makkah Mu`aẓẓamah* due to the afflictions of pain and delivery of hardship by the disbelievers.

When the people of *Madīnah* heard this news, captivating forces erupted in the heart and the eyes were overtaken by an image of celebrating a festival. The anticipation of arrival would force people away from society and into the mountains. The anticipant eyes would gaze glaringly into the path of *Makkah* as far as their eye could see. The desireful hearts would be flabbergasted by seeing anyone approaching in the distance. They would return to their homes when the sun would heat up. In this manner, several days had gone by.

One day just like every other, time passed and those in wait who would console the wishes and soothe the desires had turned back until a Jew called aloud, “O watchers of the way! Turn back! Your intent has been fulfilled! Your aspiration has been accomplished!”

Upon hearing this call, the eyes, which had just been consumed by aspirational astonishment, began to shed tears of happiness. The hearts which had wilted due to despair began to thrive with rejuvenation.

They anxiously advanced towards leadership. They selflessly carried the tidings to society.

Now what?

The hour of happiness had arrived. The wish which had been asked was fulfilled. The sounds from the hymns of happiness rose from every house.

The veiled little girls would play the *daf*. They came out singing hymns of laudation expressing joy:

طلع البدر علينا　　من ثنيات الوداع

وجب الشكر علينا　　ما دعا لله داع

The full moon rose over us | From the valleys of Wadā`
Gratitude is compulsory on us | as long as any caller calls to Allāh

Young girls from *Banū Najjār* appeared from the alleyways expressing happiness by this couplet:

نحن جوار من بنى النجار　　يا حبذا محمد من جار

We are young girls from Banū al-Najjār
Oh, what a splendid neighbor is Muḥammad!

Essentially, there was an uprising of euphoria. Joyfulness would flow from the homes and walls.

And one day is this, wherein *Madīnah* slips from the Oppressed 'Imām, Allāh Almighty is pleased with him, and not just *Madīnah*, but all the amenities and conveniences of the world take their leave one by one and bid farewell.

All these things aside, the neighboring of the pampering mother, the closeness of the full-brother, and most of all, the proximity of the Noble Grandfather, upon him be blessing and salutation, who sacrificed his own son for the 'Imām, Allāh Almighty is pleased with him.

Are these such things that one can easily turn his eyes from? How can one turn his gaze with ease?

If the 'Imām, Allāh Almighty is pleased with him, was to be assassinated for not leaving *Madīnah*, he would have accepted being assassinated and would not have stepped foot out of *Madīnah*.

However, what is the remedy for the compulsion of fate pulling the reins of the 'Imām's, Allāh Almighty is pleased with him, camel to the plain wherein destiny had made preparations for the murder of foreigners and for the martyrdom of the thirsty?

The land of *Madīnah*, upon which he crawled, which had witnessed the blossoms of his childhood, where the miracles of his adolescence had manifested, mourns in bewilderment, embraces the lovely delicate footsteps of he who travels to a foreign land, and is saying by forms of expression, "O ornament of Fāṭimah's, Allāh is pleased with her, lap! Adornment of the heart! Blossom of life! What destination have you intended? What land is it that you intend to bestow honor to by these feet of honor which are the stars of my eyes?"

اے تماشا گاہ عالم روئے تو
تو کجا بہر تماشا مے روی

Which land do you go to see
While the eyes of the world are fixed on your enlightened face?

The further this caravan of blessings distanced itself from the gaze, the more the desire of the mountains and the minarets of *Masjid Nabawī* which had been left behind became manifest to continuously rise higher and see until those who departed had vanished from the view.

An eeriness filled of yearning captivated the community of *Madīnah*.

اللهم صل على سيدنا ومولانا محمد وآله وصحبه أجمعين

O Allāh send blessings upon our master and chief, Muḥammad, and all of his offspring and companions.

Along the way, he met `Abd Allāh bin Muṭī`, Allāh Almighty is pleased with him. He said, "Where have you intended to go?"

"For now, *Makkah*."

He said, "*Kūfah* should not be intended. It is a very unprincipled city. Your honorable father was martyred there. They betrayed your brother. Do not intend to go anywhere except *Makkah*. If you are martyred, by Allāh, we will lose our position. We will all be made slaves."

Finally, His Eminence reached *Makkah* and resided safely and peacefully until the seventh of *Dhū al-Ḥijjah*.[24]

[24] *al-Kāmil fī al-Tārīkh, Dhikr al-Khabr `an Murāsalah al-Kūfiyīn, Vol. 3, Pg. 381*

10

THE MISCHIEF OF THE KUFIS AND THE MARTYRDOM OF ‘IMAM MUSLIM

When the people of *Kūfah* learned of the malicious Yazīd’s ascent to throne, the demand for pledge of allegiance from the ‘Imām, Allāh Almighty is pleased with him, and the ‘Imām’s departure from *Madīnah* to come to *Makkah*, they were reminded of their old ways of deceit and mischief. They gathered at the home of Sulaymān bin Ṣurad Khuzā`ī and after conferring, they penned the request that, “Please come and save us from the oppression of Yazīd.” Upon the collection of one hundred fifty requests, the ‘Imām, Allāh Almighty is pleased with him, wrote, “I will send my trusted paternal cousin, Muslim bin `Aqīl. If he sees your conduct to be okay and informs of it, we will come soon.”

Sayyidunā Muslim, Allāh Almighty is pleased with him, reached *Kūfah*. Here, the *Kūfis* vowed to pledge allegiance on the hand of the 'Imām, Allāh Almighty is pleased with him, and to support the 'Imām. Moreover, eighteen thousand of them had even pledged allegiance. They had satisfied Sayyidunā Muslim so much by their convincing that he wrote to the 'Imām about his coming.

Elsewhere, the *Kūfis* informed the filthy Yazīd that, "Ḥusayn has sent Muslim, and the ruler of *Kūfah*, Nu`mān bin Bashīr, Allāh is pleased with them both, deals politely with him. If you accept what is best for *Kūfah*, send an incredible oppressor like yourself."

He sent `Abd Allāh bin Ziyād as the ruler and commanded him to assassinate Muslim or to expel him from *Kūfah*. When this reprobate reached *Kūfah* and found a congregation of eighteen thousand with the 'Imām, Allāh Almighty is pleased with him, he commissioned the leaders for intimidation. They threatened some and broke others with greed, such that in a matter of no time, there remained only thirty men with 'Imām Muslim, Allāh Almighty is pleased with him.

Seeing this, Muslim exited the *masjid* to seek some place for refuge. By the time he exited the door, there remained not a single person with him.

إنا لله وإنا إليه راجعون

Indeed, to Allāh we belong and to Him we shall return.

Finally, he took shelter in a house. Learning of this, 'Ibn Ziyād sent an army. When the sounds reached 'Imām Muslim, he got up, sword in hand, and ousted those swindlers from the house.

Sometime later, they regrouped and returned. The nephew of Allāh's lion stood again with a sword in hand and put those jackals in distress in a matter of moments.

After this happened several times and those cowards were completely unable to subdue this solitary man of Allāh, they were forced to climb the roofs and began throwing stones and burning sticks.

The oppressed lion's body was covered in blood due to the stones of those oppressors, but he came out swinging, sword in hand and in a state of rage. He broke loose on the battalions that stood in the way like a punishment of torment.

Upon seeing such a state, 'Ibn 'Ash`ath said, "For you, Allāh Almighty is pleased with him, is indemnity. You shall neither be killed nor dishonored."

The oppressed Muslim, Allāh Almighty is pleased with him, became exhausted and took a seat leaning on a wall. A mule was presented for transportation. He was made to ascend it and someone took the sword from the hand of His Eminence. He said, "This is the first deceit."

'Ibn 'Ash`ath said, "Do not fear at all."

He said, "Where did that indemnity go?" and began to weep.

One individual said, "A warrior such as yourself and crying!?"

He said, "I do not cry for myself. Crying is for Ḥusayn and the family of Ḥusayn, as he should be arriving upon your convincing, and he is not informed of your deceit and treason."

Then, he said to 'Ibn 'Ash`ath, "I see that you will be incapable of providing me indemnity and your indemnity will be of no benefit. If it is possible, at least send one of your men to 'Imām Ḥusayn and inform him of my situation so that he may turn back and not fall for the deceit of the *Kūfīs*."

When Muslim, Allāh Almighty is pleased with him, was brought to the malicious 'Ibn Ziyād, 'Ibn 'Ash`ath said, "I have given him indemnity."

That scum responded, "What relation do you have with giving indemnity? We sent you to bring him. Not to give indemnity."

'Ibn 'Ash`ath remained silent. Muslim was parched due to the excessive efforts and plethora of wounds. He saw a pitcher of cold water and said, "Give me some of this to drink."

'Ibn `Amr Bāhilī said, "Do you see how cold it is? You cannot even taste a drop of it – to the point that you (*ma`ādh Allāh*, Allāh forbid) will drink the hot water in Hell."

'Imām Muslim, Allāh Almighty is pleased with him, said, "O stone-hearted and ill-mannered person! You are the one deserving of the water of *ḥamīm*[25] and the fire of Hell!"

Then, `Ammārah bin `Uqbah felt pity, called for cold water, and presented it. The 'Imām, Allāh Almighty is pleased with him, tried to drink the water, but the bowl became full of blood. This happened three times and he said, "Allāh, Himself, does not approve of it."

When he came in front of the malicious 'Ibn Ziyād, he ('Imām Muslim, Allāh Almighty is pleased with him) did not say *salām* to

[25] *Ḥamīm: a water reserved for sinners in Hell (Translator)*

him, and he ('Ibn Ziyād) became enraged saying, "You will surely be killed."

He said, "Then allow me to say my will."

He gave permission. The oppressed Muslim, Allāh Almighty is pleased with him, said to `Amr bin Sa`d, "There is a relation between you and I, and I have a private demand from you."

That stone-hearted individual said, "I do not wish to hear it."

'Ibn Ziyād said, "Listen to it. He is the son of your paternal uncle."

He took him into seclusion and he ('Imām Muslim, Allāh Almighty is pleased with him) said, "In *Kūfah*, I have taken a loan of seven hundred, pay it back. After the assassination, take my corpse from 'Ibn Ziyād and bury it. Also, send someone to 'Imām Ḥusayn, Allāh Almighty is pleased with him, to dissuade him."

'Ibn Sa`d related all these demands to 'Ibn Ziyād. He said, "At times, a trust is kept with the deceitful." This meant that he had asked for it to be kept a secret and you have revealed it.

"You have disposal of your wealth, do as you will. If Ḥusayn does not target us, we will not target him. Otherwise, we will not keep away from him. As for the corpse of Muslim, we will not pay heed to your appeal."

Then, upon receiving the command, the oppressive executioner took him above the palace and 'Imām Muslim, Allāh Almighty is pleased with him, was continuously involved in *taṣbīḥ* and *'istighfār* to the point that he was assassinated, and his blessed head was sent to Yazīd.[26]

[26] *al-Kāmil fī al-Tārīkh, Da`wah 'Ahl al-Kūfah, Vol. 3, Pg. 395-397*

11

THE ʿIMAM OF PARADISE LEAVES MAKKAH

پائی نہ تیغ عشق سے ہم نے کہیں پناہ | قرب حرم میں بھی تو ہیں قربانیوں میں ہم

We did not find refuge anywhere from the sword of love
Even in the proximity of the Ḥaram, we are in sacrifices

It is the final month of the year sixty *Hijrī* and the time of *Ḥajj*. Thousands of Muslims from distant parts of the world have come to be honored by the witnessing of their Lord's, majestic is His majesty, sacred and selected house leaving their homelands and turning from their loved ones. Happiness has stirred a passion in the hearts. Solace is swaying in the chests as this is the one night in the middle. The ninth date is in the morning, and it is the blessed day in which the result for months of labor will be reaped and the desires of ages will be fulfilled. The Muslims sacrifice themselves revolving around the *Ka`bah*.

The continuous hustle-bustle in the *Makkah Mu`aẓẓamah* has made the day a reflection of *`Eīd*, and the night, of *Laylah al-Barā'ah*. The alluring structure of the *Ka`bah* carries such tools of heart-throbbing gestures that in a crowd of thousands, whoever is seen is looking towards it with eyes full of desire. It shows that the charming manifestations of some consoling beloved are coming from the black veil after being filtered whose mind-blowing effects and heart-capturing conditions have presented the preparations for the gathering. When the devoted lovers, after having faced the afflictions of separation and the sorrows of departure, receive the opportunity of a visit in the court of their charming beloved by means of good fortune, the conflict of reverence and joy presents a propitious image of blissful nervousness in front of the eyes. They express pride in their shimmering fate in various ways and spontaneously say:

مقام وجد ہے اے دل کہ کوئے یار میں آئے ہیں | بڑے دربار میں پہنچے بڑی سرکار میں آئے

'Tis the place of ecstasy, O heart! We are in the city of the Friend
We have reached a grand palace, we have come to a grand authority

In brief, this pompous gathering has come together at the court of their Beloved for a common purpose. It is manifesting joy beyond limits at its superlative success.

However, it is evident in the sanctified countenance of the Oppressed 'Imām, Allāh Almighty is pleased with him, that he cannot remain in this gathering due to a specific reason or someone has lifted a curtain from before him, showing him such a state that his sanctified gaze does not have a chance to see this blessed view and turn his focus towards it. Even if he does look towards the gathering of the *Ḥājjīs* with longing eyes and expresses sorrow at missing the voluntary *Ḥajj*, fate says by its means of expression, "Ḥusayn! Do not be sorrowful. If there is sorrow of not performing *Ḥajj* this year, I have prepared for you the means of the Grand *Ḥajj*. Tie the *'iḥrām* of the cloth of perseverance on the waist of passion tightly. If a stream in *Makkah* has been appointed for the *sa`ī* of the *Ḥājjīs*, then a widespread field is present for you from *Makkah* to *Karbalā*. If the *Ḥājjīs* will drink the water of *Zamzam*, you will be given the refreshment of [sacred] vision after being kept thirsty for three days, so when you drink it, you will drink until you become very much satisfied. On the tenth of *`Eīd al-'Aḍḥā*, the *Ḥājjīs* will sacrifice animals in *Makkah*. So, on the tenth of *Muḥarram*, you will see those you raised in your lap suffering in soil and blood in the plain of *Karbalā*. The *Ḥājjīs* have spent wealth in the way of *Makkah*. In the plain of *Karbalā*, you will give away your life and all your life earnings. The tradesmen have opened a market for the *Ḥājjīs* in *Makkah*. You will open your shops on the riverbank of the Euphrates for the sake of the Friend. Here, the traders sell goods. There, you will sell lives. Here, the *Ḥājjīs* come for buying and selling. At your shops, your Friend will be present.

He who has said beforehand:

إِنَّ ٱللَّهَ ٱشْتَرَىٰ مِنَ ٱلْمُؤْمِنِينَ أَنفُسَهُمْ وَأَمْوَٰلَهُم بِأَنَّ لَهُمُ ٱلْجَنَّةَ

Indeed, Allāh has purchased from the believers their lives and their wealth as for them is Paradise [in exchange].[27]

In other words, these conditions have made him so immersed in the matter that the Lofty-Stationed 'Imām, Allāh Almighty is pleased with him, has intended journeying to *Kūfah* on the eighth date of `*Eīd al-'Aḍḥā*. When this news became widespread, `Umar bin `Abd al-Raḥmān, Allāh Almighty is pleased with him, opposed this intention and stood as an obstacle to the departure. He responded, "Whatever is to happen, shall surely happen."

`Abd Allāh 'ibn `Abbās, Allāh Almighty is pleased with them both, attempted to deter him with utmost humility and said, "Contemplate for a few days and wait. If the *Kūfis* kill 'Ibn Ziyād and eject and banish the enemies, then be sure that they call with goodwill. If he is in control of them and the enemies are present, they surely do not call His Eminence towards good. I suspect that those who are inviting will themselves stand in opposition."

He responded, "I will perform *'istikhārah*."

`Abd Allāh 'ibn `Abbās, Allāh Almighty is pleased with them both, came again and said, "Brother, I wish to be patient, but I am unable to do so. I fear your martyrdom in this journey. The people of Iraq are disloyal. They assassinated your father. They did not support your brother. You are the master of the people in

[27] *The Glorious Qur'ān, Sūrah: al-Tawbah: 111*

Arabia. Remain in Arabia itself or write to the people of Iraq that they eject 'Ibn Ziyād. If this happens, then go, and if you are to leave anyways, intend journeying to Yemen as there are forts there. There are valleys. That country has vast land."

He said, "Brother, by Allāh, I consider you to be an affectionate advisor, but I have made a firm intention."

He requested, "Then do not take the women and children along."

Even this was not accepted. `Abd Allāh 'ibn `Abbās, Allāh Almighty is pleased with them both, began to weep saying, "O beloved! O beloved!"

Likewise, `Abd Allāh 'ibn `Umar dissuaded him – he did not accept. He kissed the blessed forehead and said, "O one to be martyred, I entrust you to Allāh, the Sublime and the Majestic."

Similarly, `Abd Allāh 'ibn Zubayr, Allāh Almighty is pleased with them both, attempted to prevent him. He said, "I have heard from my noble father that *Makkah* will be dishonored due to a ram. I do not prefer that I become that ram."

When he departed, he received a letter along the way from his paternal cousin, Sayyidunā `Abd Allāh 'ibn Sayyidunā Ja`far Ṭayyār, Allāh Almighty is pleased with them both. It read, "Wait for a while. I am on my way to join you."

Sayyidunā `Abd Allāh, Allāh Almighty is pleased with him, requested a letter of indemnity and return from `Amr bin Sa`īd, the governor of *Makkah*, for the Oppressed 'Imām, Allāh Almighty is pleased with him. He issued it and sent his brother, Yaḥyā bin Sa`īd, along to bring him back.

The both of them arrived and went to great lengths insisting that he return. It was not accepted. He said, "I have seen the Messenger of Allāh, may Allāh Almighty send blessings and salutations upon him and his progeny, in my dream, and I have been given a command. I will fulfill it. Whether the head goes or stays."

He asked, "What was that dream?"

He responded, "I will not tell it to anyone for as long as I live."

He said this and departed.[28]

[28] *al-Kāmil fī al-Tārīkh, Dhikr Masīr al-Ḥusayn 'ilā al-Kūfah, Vol. 3, Pg. 399 (Summarized)*

12

POEM BY
`ABD AL-QADIR BEDIL DEHLAWI

سب نے عرض کی کہ شہزادۂ حیدر مت جا
اے حسین ابن علی سبط پیمبر مت جا

Everyone requested, Prince of Ḥaydar, do not go
O Ḥusayn, Son of `Alī, Grandson of the Messenger, do not go

صدمے واں پہنچے علی اور حسن کو کیا کیا
جانا کوفہ کا تو ہرگز نہیں بہتر مت جا

How many a sorrow reached `Alī and Ḥasan there
Going to Kūfah is surely not preferable, do not go

حق نما آئینہ ہے رخ ترا اندھے ہیں وہی
لے کے اندھوں میں یہ آئینہ سکندر مت جا

Your face is a mirror of truth – blind are they
Taking this mirror amongst the blind, O Victor do not go

سنگِ باراں سے بچا جامِ بلوریں اپنا | ایسے لوگوں میں جو پتھر سے ہیں بدتر مت جا

Save your crystal glass from the pelting of stones
Amongst those worse than stones, do not go

گلِ شادابِ نبی اپنے چمن سے نہ نکل | نازنیں پھول ہے تُو کانٹوں کے اندر مت جا

O blooming flower of the Prophet, do not leave your garden
You are a blooming flower, amongst the thorns, do not go

چلتے ہیں صرصرِ آفات کے مظلم جھونکے | شمع رُو قلعۂ فانوس سے باہر مت جا

The oppressive gusts of affliction blow
Candlelit face, outside the fort of the chandelier, do not go

بُوسعید ابنِ عمر جابر و ابنِ عباس | تھا یہی کلمہ سب اصحاب کے لب پر مت جا

'Abū Sa`īd, 'Ibn `Umar, Jābir, and 'Ibn `Abbās
This same phrase was on the lips of all the Companions, do not go

بیدلؔ اس شاہ کو مقتل میں قضا لے ہی گئی | کہتے سب رہ گئے اے دین کے سرور مت جا

At last, fate took this king to the battlefield, Bedil
All were left saying, "O Master of the Religion, do not go!"

When the news of the 'Imām's departure reached the 'Imām's brother, 'Imām Muḥammad bin Ḥanafīyah, Allāh Almighty is pleased with him, he was performing *wuḍū'* in a basin. He cried so much that he filled the basin with tears. When the 'Imām had traveled a short distance, he met the poet, Farazdaq, coming from *Kūfah*. He was asked about the condition of the *Kūfīs*.

He responded, "O part of Rasūl Allāh's, Allāh Almighty send blessings and salutations upon him and his progeny, heart! Their hearts are with His Eminence. Their swords are with *Banū 'Umayyah*. The decree descends from the sky, and Allāh does what He wills."

13

OBSTRUCTION FROM 'IBN ZIYAD

In short, there the 'Imām, Allāh Almighty is pleased with him, departed, and here the news reached the malicious individual and cause of corruption, 'Ibn Ziyād. He had blockades put into place by the army from *Qādisīyah* to *Khifān*, the mountain of *La`la`*, and *Quṭquṭānah*. Thus, he laid the foundation for the piercing of the hearts of the Muslims and the placement of a wound in the liver until the Day of Resurrection.

The Oppressed 'Imām, Allāh Almighty is pleased with him, sent Qays bin Mus-hir to *Kūfah* to give notice of his arrival. When this individual enveloped in mercy reached *Qādisīyah*, 'Ibn Ziyād's officers arrested him and took him to that malicious being. That outcast said, "If you desire the best for your life, get on this roof and hurl slurs at Ḥusayn."

Upon hearing this, this bearer of sacrifice for the Prophetic Household, the admirer of the Messenger's *'Ahl al-Bayt*, ascended the roof and following the praise and glorification of Allāh, blessed and exalted is He, he began to roar, "Today, Ḥusayn is superior to all the world. He is a piece of the heart of Rasūl Allāh's, may Allāh Almighty send blessings and salutations upon him and his progeny, princess, Fāṭimah Zahrā, Allāh Almighty is pleased with her. He is the light of Mawlā `Alī's, Allāh Almighty is pleased with him, eyes, the pleasure of his heart. I am his delegate. Obey his command and follow him!"

He then said, "Curse be upon 'Ibn Ziyād and his father."

Eventually, that coward became enraged and ordered that he be dropped from the roof and martyred.[29]

At this time, the anxious heart of the one intoxicated by a cup of love turned its face to the `*Arsh*-Stationed 'Imām in a pleading manner saying:

بجرم عشق توام مے کشند غوغائیست | تو نیز بر سر بام آکہ خوش تماشائیست

They murder me for the crime of your love – hence, the uproar
You come and see on the roof too, 'tis a beautiful sight

[29] *al-Kāmil fī al-Tārīkh, Dhikr Masīr al-Ḥusayn 'ilā al-Kūfah, Vol. 3, Pg. 402*

14

THE COMPANIONSHIP OF ZUHAYR BIN QAYN BAJALI

رضي الله عنه

As the Oppressed 'Imām, Allāh Almighty is pleased with him, moved forward, he met Zuhayr bin Qayn Bajalī, Allāh Almighty is pleased with him, along the way. He was returning from *Ḥajj* and harbored some resentment with Mawlā `Alī, Allāh Almighty is pleased with him. He would spend all day with the 'Imām and spend the night away.

One day, the 'Imām had him called for and so he came begrudgingly. Allāh knows what was said and which of the graceful mannerisms it was that snatched his heart. Now that he had come back, he placed his luggage amongst the luggage of the 'Imām, Allāh Almighty is pleased with him, and said to his companions, "Whoever wishes to stay with me, stay. Otherwise, this meeting is the final meeting."

Thereafter, he explained the reason for him bringing his luggage and joining the 'Imām, Allāh Almighty is pleased with him, "When we battled the city of *Balanjar*, it was conquered. We were very delighted upon the receipt of abundant war-booty. Sayyidunā Salmān Fārisī, Allāh Almighty is pleased with him, said, 'When you encounter the master of the youth of Muḥammad's, may Allāh Almighty send blessings and salutations upon him, household, be even more delighted than this as you battle the enemy alongside him.' Now that time has come. I entrust you all to Allāh."

He then divorced his wife and said, "Go home. I do not wish for any harm to come to you because of me." [30]

Allāh knows the allure of which doomsday has been placed in the graceful mannerisms of these beautiful people. Whoever they bestow with a gaze breaks down from every angle and eventually becomes theirs. Then, neither the friendships of the friends remain, nor the closeness of the wife or child.

After all, this is the same Zuhayr who harbored resentment for Mawlā `Alī, Allāh Almighty is pleased with him, and would stay apart from the 'Imām at night. What has happened to him? Whose graceful mannerism has restrained him such that, let alone the company of his loved ones, he felt obliged to divorce his wife, give his life in a state of helplessness, and became prepared to be martyred after facing difficulties?

[30] *al-Kāmil fī al-Tārīkh, Dhikr Masīr al-Ḥusayn 'ilā al-Kūfah, Vol. 3, Pg. 403*

15

THE NEWS OF ‘IMAM MUSLIM’S MARTYRDOM ﵁

Now, as this caravan moved along, they encountered a man sent by ‘Ibn ‘Ash`ath who was sent with the purpose of fulfilling the bequest of Sayyidunā Muslim, Allāh Almighty is pleased with him. Upon learning the news of Sayyidunā Muslim’s, Allāh Almighty is pleased with him, martyrdom from him, some of the companions implored the ‘Imām by oath to return from this very point.

The loved ones of the martyred Muslim, Allāh Almighty is pleased with him, said, “We cannot turn back at any cost. We will either avenge the unrightful bloodshed or we will go meet the late Muslim, Allāh Almighty is pleased with him.” The ‘Imām said, “Life after you is in vain.”

Then, he said to those who joined him along the way, "The *Kūfis* have spared us. Now, whoever wishes can turn back. Nothing will be bothersome to us."

He said this because the people accompanied him under the impression that the 'Imām was traveling to a place wherein the people have already pledged allegiance. Hearing this, apart from the few saints of Allāh that were fortunate enough to accompany him in travel from *Makkah Mu`aẓẓamah,* everyone went along their way. Thereafter, another Arab was encountered.

He requested, "Now, it is going on sword and spearhead. You are implored by oath: turn back."

He responded, "Whatever Allāh wills inevitably occurs."[31]

[31] *al-Kāmil fi al-Tārīkh, Dhikr Masīr al-Ḥusayn 'ilā al-Kūfah, Vol. 3, Pg. 403 (Summarized)*

16

THE ARRIVAL OF SAYYIDUNA HURR

رضي الله عنه

Now, the Lofty-Stationed 'Imām, Allāh Almighty is pleased with him, has surpassed the station of *Sharāf*. It is the afternoon. Suddenly, one companion exclaimed in a loud voice, "*Allāhu 'Akbar*!"

He said, "What is it?"

He responded, "Date trees can be seen."

Two individuals from the clan of *Banū 'Asad* said, "There were never dates in this land."

He said, "Then what is it?"

They responded, "There seem to be horsemen."

He said, "My thoughts are the same. Okay, so is there any place of refuge here which we can take on our backs to battle the enemy with complacency?"

He responded, "Yes! There is the mountain, *Dhū Ḥusam,* if His Eminence reaches it before them."

The conversations were just taking place when the horsemen were spotted.

The 'Imām, Allāh Almighty is pleased with him, took precedence and advanced towards the mountain.

When they came even closer, they learned that it was Ḥurr who was made an officer over one thousand individuals of the cavalry to take the 'Imām, Allāh Almighty is pleased with him, to the malicious 'Ibn Ziyād.

Right on this afternoon, he dismounted in front of the 'Imām's companions. The son of *Kawthar's* Owner commanded, "Give water to them and their horses."

The companions of the 'Imām, Allāh Almighty is pleased with them, gave them water. When the time of *Ẓuhr* came, the 'Imām commanded the *mu'adh-dhin* for the *'adhān* and said to those people, "My coming to you was not by my own will. You invited me by continuously sending letters and delegates. Now, if you testify to accord, I will come to your city. Otherwise, I will return."

No one responded and he said to the *mu'adh-dhin,* "Say the *'iqāmah.*"

The 'Imām, Allāh Almighty is pleased with him, asked Ḥurr, "Will you lead your companions in *ṣalāh*?"

He responded, "No. You lead, and we will all follow."

Following *ṣalāh,* Ḥurr went to his station. The 'Imām, Allāh Almighty is pleased with him, said to those people after the praise of Allāh Almighty, "If you fear Allāh, sublime and majestic is He, and recognize the right to be for the deserving, then the pleasure of Allāh is solely in us, the *'Ahl al-Bayt,* being deserving of the authoritative position as opposed to those oppressors.

Despite this, if you dislike us, do not recognize our right, and wish to hold views of us contrary to your letters and delegates, then I will turn back."

Ḥurr responded, "By Allāh! We do not know of any such letter or delegate." The 'Imām took out two saddlebags full of letters and presented them.

Ḥurr said, "I am not of those who sent letters. I have been given the command that when I encounter you, Allāh Almighty is pleased with him, I deliver you to 'Ibn Ziyād in *Kūfah.*"

He responded, "Your death is near, and this intent is distant."

Then, he ordered his companions, "Let's go back."

Ḥurr stopped him. He (the 'Imām) said, "May your mother mourn for you. What do you want?"

He responded, "Listen! By Allāh, if anyone in all of Arabia said this besides you, I would say the same to his mother no matter who it is. But, by Allāh, I cannot utter the sanctified name of your mother in such circumstances."

The 'Imām responded, "What do you want, after all?"

He said, "To take His Eminence to 'Ibn Ziyād."

He responded, "Then, by Allāh! I will not go with you."

He said, "Then, by Allāh! I will not leave you."

When the matter escalated and Ḥurr saw that the 'Imām, Allāh Almighty is pleased with him, would not be pleased in this manner and his faith did not permit the association of any blasphemy, he said, "I cannot separate from His Eminence in all of the daytime. However, when the evening comes, stay separately giving the excuse of the companionship of women. At any time in the night, find an opportunity and leave. I will write and send something to 'Ibn Ziyād. Perhaps, Allāh Almighty makes the scenario that I do not dare to fall into an improper affair." [32]

[32] *al-Kāmil fī al-Tārīkh, Thumma Dakhalat Sanah 'Iḥdā wa Sittīn, Vol. 3, Pg. 407 (Summarized)*

17

THE DISLOYALTY OF THE KUFIS AND NEWS OF THE MARTYRDOM OF QAYS BIN MUS-HIR

When they reached *`Udhayb al-Hijānāt,* they encountered four individuals coming from *Kūfah*. They asked regarding the situation and Majma` bin `Ubayd Allāh `Āmirī responded, "The leaders of the city have been bent by heavy bribes and their pouches have been filled with wealth. Thus, they have unanimously become opposed to His Eminence. As for the commoners, their hearts are inclined towards His Eminence, Allāh Almighty is pleased with him, and the swords of those very people shall be extended towards His Eminence in the coming day."

He said, "What is the state of my delegate, Qays?"

He replied, "He was murdered."

The 'Imām, Allāh Almighty is pleased with him, began to cry beyond control and said, "Some have fulfilled their vow and others are in wait. My Allāh! Gather us and him in Paradise!"

Ṭirimmāḥ bin `Adī said, "The men with you are numbered. Even if the unit of Ḥurr battles you, it would suffice – never mind the unit I saw in *Kūfah* a day before leaving which is prepared to come towards you, Allāh Almighty is pleased with him. I have never seen such a massive military unit in all my life. I implore His Eminence by oath – if there exists the possibility of even a hand-span of distance from them, then do just that much. However, if you would be pleased by a place wherein, by the permission of Allāh Almighty, you can reside with peace and satisfaction and plan, then come with me towards Mount *'Ājā'*. By Allāh! Due to that mountain, we were safeguarded against the attacks of the kings of *Ghusān* and *Ḥumayr* and Nu`mān bin al-Mundhir. Rather, [we were safeguarded against the attacks] of all of Arabia and non-Arabia. Your Eminence, stay there and command the residents of *'Ājā'* and *Sullamī*. By Allāh, not even ten days will pass and the cavalry and the infantry of the *Ṭay'* nation will present themselves in service. Then, as long as the blessed intention is for, stay amongst us, and if there is an intent to advance, then it is my responsibility to commission into the company of His Eminence twenty thousand youth of the *Banū Ṭay'* who shall swing their swords before His Eminence, and as long as even the power to blink remains in them, the enemy will not be able to approach His Eminence."

He responded, "May Allāh reward you. We have had some words with the *Kūfīs* which we cannot turn on."

He said this and granted him leave.[33]

[33] *al-Kāmil fī al-Tārīkh, Thumma Dakhalat Sanah 'Iḥdā wa Sittīn, Vol. 3, Pg. 409 (Summarized)*

18

THE DREAM OF THE LOFTY RANKED 'IMAM ﷺ

Along the way, the 'Imām saw a dream and he woke up saying:

إنا لله وإنا إليه راجعون والحمد لله رب العالمين

"Verily, we belong to Allāh and to Him we shall return. All praise is to Allāh, the Lord of all Worlds."

'Imām Zayn al-`Ābidīn, Allāh Almighty is pleased with him, said, "O my father, may I be sacrificed upon you. What did you see?" He responded, "I saw a cavalier in a dream. He was saying, 'People walk, and their death follows them.' I have understood that we are being informed of our murder."

Sayyidunā `Ābid, Allāh Almighty is pleased with him, said, "May Allāh not show you any evil. Are we not on the truth?"

He responded, "We surely are."

He said, "If we give our lives and sacrifice ourselves for the truth, then what is the worry?"

He replied, "May Allāh give you a reward superior to any reward ever given to any son on behalf of any father." [34]

[34] *al-Kāmil fī al-Tārīkh, Thumma Dakhalat Sanah 'Iḥdā wa Sittīn, Vol. 3, Pg. 411 (Summarized)*

19

THE COMMAND OF CRUELTY ON THE `ARSH-STATIONED ‘IMAM FROM ‘IBN ZIYAD

When they reached Nineveh, they met a horseman coming from *Kūfah*. He delivered a letter of ‘Ibn Ziyād to Ḥurr. It read, “Be stern with Ḥusayn, wherever he descends, he should descend onto a plain and reside away from water. This delegate will continuously accompany you such that he will inform me how you have executed my command.”

After reading the letter, Ḥurr said to the ‘Imām, “This is the command I have received. I cannot oppose it as this delegate has been sent being made a spy on me.”

Zuhayr bin Qayn said, “By Allāh! Whatever comes after this will be much crueler than this. Battling this unit is easier for us than battling those who will come in the future.”

He said, “We will not start it.”

These talks were ongoing when the sun set and the moon of *Muḥarram's* second night began showing its very subtle glow. Both camps stayed separately.[35]

[35] *al-Kāmil fī al-Tārīkh, Thumma Dakhalat Sanah 'Iḥdā wa Sittīn, Vol. 3, Pg.* 411 *(Summarized)*

20

THE DEPARTURE OF THE PROPHET'S GRANDSON IN THE NIGHT

Now, the darkness rises from the eastern horizons and the lanterns of the celestial congregation continue to ignite. The dwellers of the universal atmosphere and freed creation of Allāh, the birds, have grown silent after much singing.

The clock that tells the speed of time and the calendar that explains the calculation of ages, the establishment of the 'Islāmic year which the magnificent hand of nature has stretched to the extent of *`urjūn qadīm,*[36] conceals itself after giving glimpses of alluring mannerisms.

[36] *`Urjūn Qadīm is literally defined as an old branch of a date tree. In the 39th verse of Sūrah Yāsīn, the Qur'ān mentions this as an example of the state that the moon will ultimately resort to. (Translator)*

The colors of darkness have deepened even more. That gaze which could sight items afar in the vast population of the world with complete satisfaction and identify them approximately two hours earlier, now struggles, rather fails, to deliver benefit in even this minute distance.

Moreover, even if something is sighted, the black veil of the night prevents its ascertainment. The excessive passing of time and the halting of all talks and walks have produced eeriness; the night has become even more gruesome.

The gaze of the stars that spend the night awake is lowered. The sleepers are sleeping blanketed in utmost satisfaction. Slumber has worked its magic on the era. The sounds of slumber have emerged from Ḥurr's camp.

The Heaven-Bound 'Imām, who has spent this much of the night awake awaiting this very opportunity, is making preparations for departure. The provisions which had been packed since the evening were loaded. The women and children were mounted.

Now, this sanctified caravan departs in this dark night dependent solely on the hope that it is late into the night, the foes shall remain asleep, and we will have traveled a great distance from them before morning arrives. The remainder of the night is spent in travel and speeding the animals up.

21

ARRIVAL IN THE PLAIN OF KARBALA

Now witness the wonders of fate. The oppressed meet with morning, but where? In the plain of *Karbalā*.

It is the second day of *Muḥarram*, sixty-one *Hijrī*, and it is a Thursday.

\`Amr bin Sa\`d has arrived at the opposition of the 'Imām along with his military unit. The malicious 'Ibn Ziyād had commissioned that wretched individual to battle the Daylamite heathens and he had also written the sanction of [his] governing Ray in return for the victory. However, when he received news of the Oppressed 'Imām, it fell on the ill will of the ill-fated being. He summoned him and said, "Keep the intent for over there postponed. First, face Ḥusayn. Go there after you are done."

He responded, "Excuse me."

He said, "Fine, but on the condition that you return our sanction."

He sought one day of respite and discussed with loved ones. Everyone protested and his nephew, Ḥamzah bin Mughīrah bin Shu`bah, said, "O maternal uncle! I implore you by the oath of Allāh! Do not sin by opposing Ḥusayn! By Allāh! If all of the world is in your governance, abandoning it is easier than you meeting Allāh as the murderer of Ḥusayn!"

He responded, "I will not go."

However, hesitation remained in the impure heart. There came a sound at night – someone was saying:

أأترك ملك الري والري رغبة	أم أرجع مذموما بقتل حسين
وفي قتله النار التي ليس دونها	حجاب وملك الري قرة عين

He said, "Shall I abandon the rule of Ray while Ray is so desirable? Or shall I endure the blame of Ḥusayn's, Allāh Almighty is pleased with him, murder while in his murder is a fire which has no hindrance and the rule of Ray is the coolness of the eye?" [37]

[37] *al-Kāmil fī al-Tārīkh, Thumma Dakhalat Sanah 'Iḥdā wa Sittīn, Vol. 3, Pg. 412 (Summarized)*

22

WITHHOLDING WATER FROM THE OPPRESSED 'IMAM

رضي الله عنه

Ultimately, the will found assurance in the assassination of the Oppressed 'Imām.

The irreligious being had proved to be in accordance with:

الدين مزرعة الدنيا

The religion is the cultivation of the world.

Water was hindered from the son of *Kawthar's* Distributor, may Allāh Almighty send blessings and salutations upon him and his progeny, by sending five hundred horsemen to the riverbanks of the Euphrates.

One night the 'Imām had him sent for. He presented himself in the middle of both camps. Discussions lasted for an extended period of time.

The 'Imām explained, "Abandon siding with the people of corruption."

He said, "My home will be demolished."

He responded, "I will have a better one built."

He said, "My property will be seized."

He replied, "I will grant you one even better than it." [38]

[38] *al-Kāmil fī al-Tārīkh, Thumma Dakhalat Sanah 'Iḥdā wa Sittīn, Vol. 3, Pg. 413 (Summarized)*

23

‘IBN SA`D’S LETTER TO ‘IBN ZIYAD AND SHIMR’S INCITING AGAINST THE ‘IMAM

These discussions lasted for three or four nights. The result of this was this much that ‘Ibn Sa`d wrote a treaty-like letter to ‘Ibn Ziyād saying, “Ḥusayn wants that he either go back, to Yazīd, or to any ‘Islāmic frontier. Your desire is fulfilled in this,” even though the ‘Imām certainly did not say to go to the filthy Yazīd.

‘Ibn Ziyād read the letter and said, “It is fine.”

The wretched Shimr Dhū al-Jawshan said, “Does he obey any commands? By Allāh, if Ḥusayn [Allāh Almighty is pleased with him] leaves without obeying you, there is honor and power for him, and for your sake is weakness and disgrace. Not like this. Rather, he must go by your command. If you give punishment, then you are the master, and if you forgive, it is your favor. I have heard that discussions go on lasting entire nights amongst Ḥusayn and 'Ibn Sa`d."

'Ibn Ziyād responded, "Your opinion is suitable. You take my letter to 'Ibn Sa`d. If he obeys, then be obedient to him. Otherwise, you are the commander of the unit, and take off 'Ibn Sa`d's head and send it to me."

Then he wrote to 'Ibn Sa`d, "Did I send you to Ḥusayn so you can take his hand, give hope and leeway, or be his advocate? Look! Order Ḥusayn for my obedience. If he accepts, send him here as a follower. Otherwise, massacre him and his companions. If you obey our command, you will be given reward for obedience. Otherwise, leave our unit to Shimr."

When Shimr took the letter, `Abd Allāh 'ibn 'Abū al-Maḥl bin Ḥizām was with him. His paternal aunt, 'Umm al-Banīn bint Ḥizām, was the wife of Mawlā `Alī, may Allāh ennoble his countenance, and the mother of the sons of Mawlā `Alī, Sayyidunā `Abbās, `Uthmān, `Abd Allāh, and Ja`far. He sought indemnity from 'Ibn Ziyād for his paternal aunt's sons and he thus issued it. He sent that letter to those gentlemen, and they responded, "We have no need of your indemnity. The protection of Allāh Almighty is superior to the protection of 'Ibn Sumayyah."[39]

[39] *al-Kāmil fī al-Tārīkh, Thumma Dakhalat Sanah 'Iḥdā wa Sittīn, Vol. 3, Pg. 414 (Summarized)*

24

SHIMR'S ARRIVAL TO 'IBN SA`D

When Shimr delivered the letter of the malicious 'Ibn Ziyād to 'Ibn Sa`d, he said, "Damn you! I suspect that you have ruined the matter by steering 'Ibn Ziyād away from acting on my letter. I had complete hope of a settlement taking place. Ḥusayn will, in no way, accept obedience. By Allāh, his father's heart is kept in his chest!" Shimr responded, "Now what do you will to do?" He said, "What 'Ibn Ziyād has written." Shimr called `Abbās and his full-brothers and said, "O nephews! You have indemnity!" They responded, "May the curse of Allāh be on you and your indemnity! You act as a maternal uncle and give us indemnity, while there is no indemnity for the son of Allāh's Messenger, may Allāh Almighty send blessings and salutations upon him and his progeny?" [40]

[40] *al-Kāmil fi al-Tārīkh, Vol. 3, Pg. 414 (Summarized)*

25

THE ARRIVAL OF THE NOBLE GRANDFATHER IN A DREAM

May Allāh Almighty Send Blessings and Salutations Upon Him and His Progeny

It is the eve of Thursday and the ninth date of *Muḥarram*, sixty-one *Hijrī*. At this time, the Hell-bound unit has been given movement in opposition of the Master of the Youth in Paradise. The one intoxicated by the wine of martyrdom, the lion of the *Ḥaydarī* den, is present in front of the pure tent, sword in hand.

He has caught a wink and sees his Noble Grandfather, upon him be blessing and salutation, in a dream. He has placed the sanctified hand on the chest of his dear child saying:

اللهم اعط الحسين صبرا وأجرا

O Allāh, grant Ḥusayn patience and reward!

Furthermore, he says, "Now you will meet us soon and will open your fast after coming to us."

The 'Imām's eyes open in the eruption of delight. He sees the enemies are intending to attack. The 'Imām sought respite of one night bearing *Jumu`ah* in mind and intending to give bequests to the survivors.

'Ibn Sa`d sought advice. `Amr bin Ḥajjāj Zubaydī said, "Had the Daylamite heathens sought respite of one night, it should have been given." In conclusion, respite was given.[41]

[41] *al-Kāmil fī al-Tārīkh, Thumma Dakhalat Sanah 'Iḥdā wa Sittīn, Vol. 3, Pg. 415 (Summarized)*

26

THE CAMP OF THE LOFTY-STATIONED ʿIMAM PREPARING FOR BATTLE

The steps taken here were that all the tents were brought close together, and the ropes and cables were put together. A trench was dug behind the tents which was filled with reed, various materials, and dry wood.

Now, upon completing these tasks, the Muslims present themselves in the service of the ʿImām, and the ʿImām is saying to his family and companions, "In the morning, we are to encounter the enemy. I have given you all permission with complete happiness. The night remains, wherever you find an opening, leave, and each individual take with yourself one member from the people of my household. May Allāh reward you all. Disperse in the villages and cities until Allāh Almighty dismisses the affliction. When the enemy finds me, they will not pursue you."

Hearing this, the brothers, sons, and nephews of the 'Imām and the sons of `Abd Allāh 'ibn Ja`far said, "Why shall we do this? So that we can live after you? May Allāh not show us that ominous day in which you are absent and we remain."

He said to the brothers of the martyred Muslim, Allāh Almighty is pleased with him, "Muslim being assassinated is sufficient for you. I give you permission, you go."

They responded, "And what shall we say to the people when we go? Shall we say, 'We have left our ruler, our master, our most superior brother, in the trap of the enemy. Neither did we shoot arrows with him, nor did we strike a spear or swing a sword. We do not know what he endured after our leaving'? By Allāh, we will certainly not do this. Rather, we will sacrifice our lives and our children at your feet. We will sacrifice ourselves for you and die. May Allāh doom the life which is after you."

خوشا حالے کہ گردم گرد کویت | رخے بر خوں گریباں پارہ پارہ

How wonderful would it be when I wander about your lane,
In the condition that my face be bloody, and my collar in shreds.

Muslim bin `Awsajah 'Asadī said, "Should we leave His Eminence while we have yet to fulfill any right of His Eminence to create room for pardon in the court of Allāh? By Allāh, I, for one, would not leave your side to the degree that I break my spear in the chests of the enemies and as long as the sword is in my hand, I keep attacking. Allāh is a witness, even if I did not have any weapons, I would pelt stones until I am killed alongside you."

The remainder of the companions all responded in the same fashion. May Allāh, the Sublime and the Majestic, reward them all.[42] May He grant them the companionship of the Lofty-Stationed 'Imām, Allāh Almighty is pleased with him, and the shade of his Noble Grandfather, upon him be blessing and salutation, in the *Jannāt al-Firdaws*. May He grant us the honor of their blessings in the world, the hereafter, the grave, and the grand assembly.

آمین آمین یا أرحم الراحمین

'Āmīn, 'Āmīn, O Most Merciful of the merciful!

This very night, the 'Imām, Allāh Almighty is pleased with him, recited such poetry whose content drags an image of astonishment and helplessness into the eyes. Day and night, Allāh knows how many friends and loved ones time kills, and whoever it wants to kill, it will not be pleased in exchanging them for another.

The heart-rending voice which informs of the forthcoming event reaches the ear of Lady Zaynab, Allāh Almighty is pleased with her. She could not express patience.

She becomes anxious and runs screaming, "If only I had been given death before this day! Today, my mother Fāṭimah passes away! Today, my father `Alī leaves the world! Today, my brother

[42] *al-Kāmil fī al-Tārīkh, Thumma Dakhalat Sanah 'Iḥdā wa Sittīn, Vol. 3, Pg. 414 (Summarized)*

Ḥasan's funeral departs! O Ḥusayn! O souvenir of the predecessors and refuge of the survivors!"

She then fainted and fell.

Allāhu 'Akbar! Today, in the home of *Kawthar's* Owner, there is not even water sufficient to be sprinkled on the face of the unconscious sister.

When she regained consciousness, he said, "O sister, fear Allāh and be patient. Know that all the ones of the land must die, and all the ones of the sky must pass. Besides Allāh, there is an end for everyone. My father, my mother, and my brother, Allāh Almighty is pleased with them, were better than me. Every Muslim should tread the path of Allāh's Messenger, may Allāh Almighty send blessings and salutations upon him and his progeny." [43]

[43] *al-Kāmil fī al-Tārīkh, Thumma Dakhalat Sanah 'Iḥdā wa Sittīn, Vol. 3, Pg. 416 (Summarized)*

27

HERE COMES DOOMSDAY

بہاروں پر ہیں آج آرائشیں گلزارِ جنت کی
سواری آنے والی ہے شہیدانِ محبت کی

Today, the embellishments of the garden of Paradise are flourishing
The caravan of the martyrs of love is soon to arrive

کھلے ہیں گل بہاروں پر ہے پھلواری جراحت کی
فضا ہر زخم کے دامن سے وابستہ ہے جنت کی

Upon the springs, flowers have blossomed, there is a bed of wounds
An ambience of Paradise is attached to the kilt of every wound

گلا کٹوا کے بیڑی کاٹنے آئے ہیں اُمت کی
کوئی تقدیر تو دیکھے اسیرانِ مصیبت کی

They have come to break the shackles of the nation after having their throats slit
Someone take a look at the fate of the captives of affliction

شہیدِ ناز کی تفریح زخموں سے نہ کیوں کر ہو
ہوائیں آتی ہیں ان کھڑکیوں سے باغِ جنت کی

Why shall the martyr of love not take pleasure in wounds?
From those windows come breezes from the garden of Paradise

کرم والوں نے دَر کھولا تو رحمت کا سماں باندھا
کمر باندھی تو قسمت کھول دی فضل شہادت کی

When those of nobility opened the door, they created an atmosphere of mercy
When they became adamant, it unraveled the fate of the virtue of martyrdom

علی کے پیارے خاتونِ قیامت کے جگر پارے
زمیں سے آسماں تک دھوم ہے اِن کی سیادت کی

The beloved of `Alī, a piece from the heart of the Lady of the Hereafter
From land to the skies, there is a parade of his mastery

زمین کربلا پر آج مجمع ہے حسینوں کا
جمی ہے انجمن روشن ہیں شمعیں نور و ظلمت\طلعت کی

On the land of Karbalā, there is a gathering of the beautiful today
An assembly has been established, lanterns of light and darkness/rising have been ignited

یہ وہ شمعیں نہیں جو پھونک دیں اپنے فدائی کو
یہ وہ شمعیں نہیں رو کر جو کاٹیں رات آفت کی

These are not the lanterns which burn their own lovers
These are not the lanterns that pass a night of affliction sobbing

یہ وہ شمعیں ہیں جن سے جان تازہ پائیں پروانے
یہ وہ شمعیں ہیں جو ہنس کر گزاریں شب مصیبت کی

These are lanterns by which moths attain an invigorated life
These are the lanterns that spend a night of hardship in laughter

یہ وہ شمعیں نہیں جن سے فقط اک گھر منور ہو
یہ وہ شمعیں ہیں جن سے رُوح ہو کافور ظلمت کی

These are not the lanterns by which only one house is illuminated
These are the lanterns by which the spirit of darkness vanishes

دلِ حور وملائک رہ گیا حیرت زدہ ہو کر
کہ بزمِ گل رُخاں میں لے بلائیں کس کی صورت کی

The heart of the Ḥūr and Angels comes to a standstill after becoming astonished
As, in a gathering of the rose-faced, whose appearance do they sacrifice themselves for?

جدا ہوتی ہیں جانیں جسم سے جاناں سے ملتے ہیں
ہوئی ہے کربلا میں گرم مجلس وصل وفرقت کی

The lives abandon the body and meet with the beloved
In Karbalā, the gathering has been fired up of connection and separation

اسی منظر پہ ہر جانب سے لاکھوں کی نگاہیں ہیں
اسی عالم کو آنکھیں تک رہی ہیں ساری خلقت کی

Towards this very spectacle is the gaze of thousands from every direction
This very state, the eyes of the entire creation are watching

ہوا چھڑکاؤ پانی کی جگہ اشکِ یتیماں سے
بجائے فرش آنکھیں بچھ گئیں اہلِ بصیرت کی

The sprinkling was done by tears of orphans in place of water
In place of the land, the eyes of the visionaries have been spread

ہوائے یار نے پنکھے بنائے پر فرشتوں کے
سبیلیں رکھی ہیں دیدار نے خود اپنے شربت کی

The friendly breeze has turned the wings of Angels into fans
The vision has set up points of distribution for its own refreshment

اُدھر افلاک سے لائے فرشتے ہار رحمت کے

اِدھر ساغر لیے حوریں چلی آتی ہیں جنت کی

Yonder, the Angels have brought from the skies, garlands of mercy
Here, the Ḥūrs arrive having brought wine of Paradise

سجے ہیں زخم کے پھولوں سے وہ رنگین گلدستے

بہارِ خوشنمائی پر ہے صدقے رُوح جنت کی

Those colorful bouquets have been adorned by flowers of wounds
The spirit of Paradise is sacrificed on the blossom of splendor

ہوائیں گلشن فردوس سے بس بس کر آتی ہیں

نرالی عطر میں ڈوبی ہوئی ہے رُوح نکہت کی

The winds come after having settled in a garden of Paradise
The spirit of fragrance is submerged in a distinct perfume

دلِ پُر سوز کے سُلگے اگر سوز ایسی حرکت/کثرت[44] سے

کہ پہنچی عرش وطیبہ تک لپٹ سوزِ محبت کی

If the sorrow of the grieving heart is inflamed by such a movement/plethora
Then, the flame of love's sorrow reaches the `Arsh and Ṭaybah

[44] *Difference in two copies of the original text (Translator)*

ادھر چلمن اُٹھی حسنِ ازل کے پاک جلوؤں سے
ادھر چمکی تجلی بدرِ تابانِ رسالت کی

Yonder, the veil is raised from the pure manifestations of the ever-existing beauty
Here, shines the manifestation of the Glowing Moon of Messenger-hood

زمین کربلا پر آج ایسا حشر برپا ہے
کہ کھنچ کھنچ کر مٹی جاتی ہیں تصویریں قیامت کی

Such a doomsday has broken loose in the land of Karbalā today
That the images of doomsday become erased after great struggle

گھٹائیں مصطفیٰ کے چاند پر گھر گھر کر آئی ہیں
سیہ کارانِ اُمت تیرہ بختانِ شقاوت کی

Dark clouds have surrounded moon of Muṣṭafā
Of the wrongdoers of the nation, the misfortunate of ill fate

یہ کس کے خون کے پیاسے ہیں اُس کے خون کے پیاسے
بجھے گی پیاس جس سے تشنہ کامانِ قیامت کی

Whose blood are they thirsty for? Thirsty for the blood of those
From whom the thirst will be quenched of the parched on doomsday

اکیلے پر ہزاروں کے ہزاروں وار چلتے ہیں
مٹا دی دین کے ہمراہ عزت شرم و غیرت کی

Thousands of attacks from thousands are struck onto the solitary
They have erased the honor of shame and zeal surrounding the religion

مگر شیر خدا کا شیر جب بپھرا غضب آیا
پَرے ٹوٹے نظر آنے لگی صورت ہزیمت کی

But when the lion of Allāh's lion resisted, he became enraged
The [enemy] lines broke, and the face of defeat began to show

کہا یہ بوسہ دے کر ہاتھ پر جوشِ دلیری نے
بہادر آج سے کھائیں گے قسمیں اِس شجاعت کی

Giving a kiss on the hand, the passion of courage says,
"From today, the valiant will take oaths of this bravery"

تصدق ہو گئی جانِ شجاعت سچے تیور کے
فدا شیرانہ حملوں کی آدا پر روح جرأت کی

The life of courage gave itself away for the true light of sight
The spirit of bravery sacrifices itself for the mannerisms of the lion-like attacks

نہ ہوتے گر حسین ابن علی اس پیاس کے بھوکے
نکل آتی زمین کربلا سے نہر جنت کی

Had Ḥusayn 'ibn `Alī not been hungry for that thirst
A river of Paradise would have gushed forth from the land of Karbalā

مگر مقصود تھا پیاسا گلا ہی اُن کو کٹوانا
کہ خواہش پیاس سے بڑھتی رہے رُؤیت کے شربت کی

However, the intent was having a thirsty throat slit itself
So that the desire increases due to the thirst, for the refreshment of the vision

شہید ناز رکھ دیتا ہے گردن آبِ خنجر پر
جو موجیں باڑ پر آ جاتی ہیں دریائے اُلفت کی

The martyr of love places the neck on the edge of the blade
When the waves of the river of love come over the shore

یہ وقتِ زخم نکلا خون اچھل کر جسمِ اطہر سے
کہ روشن ہو گئی مشعل شبستانِ محبت کی

This blood leaps and exits from the pure body at the time of injury
As the lantern in the bedchamber of love has been ignited

سرِ بے تن تن آسانی کو شہر طیبہ میں پہنچا
تنِ بے سر کو سرداری ملی مُلکِ شہادت کی

The bodiless head reached the city of Ṭaybah for bodily peace
The headless body received kingship for the kingdom of martyrdom

حسنؔ سُنّی ہے پھر افراط و تفریط اِس سے کیوں کر ہو
اَدب کے ساتھ رہتی ہے روش اربابِ سُنّت کی

Ḥasan is Sunnī so why shall there be any immoderation or negligence committed by him?
The manner of the people of Sunnah remains with respect

28

THE COMMENCE OF OPPRESSION ON THE PROPHETIC HOUSEHOLD

The agony comes the morning on the day of `*Āshūrā'*, and on the dawn of Friday, the break of doomsday shows its face.

The `*Arsh*-Stationed 'Imām, Allāh Almighty is pleased with him, appears from the pure tent and arranges his unit of seventy-two companions: thirty-two on horseback and forty on foot.

On the right side, Zuhayr bin Qayn has been made commander and on the left, Ḥabīb bin Maẓhar, Allāh Almighty is pleased with him. Sayyidunā `Abbās, Allāh Almighty is pleased with him, has been commissioned for flag-bearing. The command has been issued to ignite the branches in the trench so the enemy does not find way from there.

Following this preparation, the Paradise-Stationed 'Imām, Allāh Almighty is pleased with him, goes to attain purification in preparation for martyrdom. `Abd al-Raḥmān bin `Abd Rabbihī and Yazīd bin Ḥuṣayn Hamdānī, Allāh Almighty is pleased with them both, wait at the entrance of the tent so they can also practice this *sunnah* themselves after the 'Imām's completion. 'Ibn Ḥuṣayn mentioned some laughing matter to `Abd al-Raḥmān. He responded, "What kind of time for laughter is this?"

He said, "Allāh is a witness. My entire clan knows that even in my youth, I never had the habit of laughter. Right now, I am delighted because of that which shall soon be received. Do you see the army bent on battling us? By Allāh, the only time standing between us and the meeting of the *Ḥūrs* is of them taking their swords and coming down on us."

The Paradise-Stationed 'Imām, Allāh Almighty is pleased with him, exits, ascends the camel, and advances towards the unfortunate to explain to them one last time. He drew close and said, "O people! Listen to me and do not make haste. If you do justice, you shall attain fortune. Otherwise, gather your companions and do as you wish. I do not seek respite. My Allāh, the One who revealed the *Qur'ān* and holds the righteous as friends, is my supporter."

When this voice of the 'Imām reached the ears of his sisters, they began to cry without control. The 'Imām sent Sayyidunā `Abbās and 'Imām Zayn al-`Ābidīn to silence them and said, "By Allāh, they are to cry a lot."

He then turned to the unfortunate and began saying, "At least mention my lineage and just think about who I am. Take a look into your collar. Can you bear my assassination? Can my dishonoring be permissible for you? Am I not the grandson of your Prophet, may Allāh Almighty send blessings and salutations upon him and his progeny? Have you not heard that the Messenger of Allāh, may Allāh Almighty send blessings and salutations upon him and his progeny, has said to my brother and I, 'You two are the masters of the youth in Paradise?' Is this much not enough to prevent you from shedding my blood?"

Shimr, the coward, responded, "We do not know what you are saying."

Ḥabīb bin Maẓhar said, "Allāh, the Sublime and the Majestic, has sealed your heart. You know nothing."

The Oppressed 'Imām then said, "By Allāh, there remains no grandson of any Prophet besides me in all of the world. Tell me, did I kill any one of your men? Did I loot any wealth or wound someone? For what do you seek revenge from me after all?"

No one responded. So, he took names and said, "O Shīth bin Rab`ī! O Ḥijāz bin 'Abjar! O Qays bin 'Ash`ath! O Zayd bin al-Ḥārith! Did you not write me letters?"

Those corrupt individuals openly denied.

He said, "You surely did write them."

He then said, "O people! If you dislike me, then allow me to go back."

No one agreed to this either.

He then said, "I seek the refuge of mine and your Lord, the Sublime and the Majestic, from you stoning me, and I seek refuge from that arrogant individual who does not believe in the Day of Resurrection."

He said this and descended from the blessed camel.

Zuhayr bin Qayn moves forward on horseback wearing a weapon and begins to say, "O people of *Kūfah,* the torment of Allāh is soon to arrive. It is the right of one Muslim over another to advise him. You and I are religious brothers for now. When the sword is raised, you will be a separate group and we will be another. Allāh Almighty has tested you and I regarding the offspring of His Prophet, may Allāh Almighty send blessings and salutations upon him and his progeny, and how you and I deal with them. I call you to the support of 'Imām Ḥusayn, Allāh Almighty is pleased with him, and I seek to prevent your obedience to the transgressor, the son of a transgressor, 'Ibn Ziyād. You will not see but oppression and tyranny from him."

The *Kūfis* responded, "Until we kill you and your leader or send you to 'Ibn Ziyād having been made obedient, we will not budge from here."

Zuhayr, Allāh Almighty is pleased with him, said, "By Allāh, the son of Fāṭimah is more deserving of love and support than the son of Sumayyah. Even if you do not support him, at least do not wish for his murder."

Upon this, Shimr, the outcast, shot an arrow and said, "Shut up! You have annoyed us for too long!"

Zuhayr, Allāh Almighty is pleased with him, responded, "O son of the uncultured one who urinates on his own ankles! I am not speaking to you! You are an utter animal! I think that you may not even know two verses of the *Qur'ān*! Glad tidings to you of painful torment and dishonor on the Day of Resurrection!"

Shimr said, "In just a short while, you and your leader will be killed."

He responded, "Do you scare me with death? By Allāh, I prefer dying at his feet than living for eternity with you all!"

Then, in a loud voice, he began to say, "O people, this disrespectful and ill-mannered person deceives you and seeks to make you unaware of the true religion. Those who murder the *'Ahl al-Bayt* or their companions, by Allāh, the intercession of Muḥammad, may Allāh Almighty send blessings and salutations upon him and his progeny, will not reach them!"

The Lofty-Stationed 'Imām, Allāh Almighty is pleased with him, called him back.[45]

Now, the misfortunate 'Ibn Sa`d moved his impure unit towards the Oppressed 'Imām.

Ḥurr said, "May you receive the bashing of Allāh. Will you battle with them?"

He said, "I will battle, and I will battle them in such a manner whose minimal degree will be the heads being blown off and the falling of the hands."

He responded, "Do you not accept the three matters he put forth?"

He said, "If I had the power, I would accept them." [46]

[45] *al-Kāmil fī al-Tārīkh, Thumma Dakhalat Sanah 'Iḥdā wa Sittīn, Vol. 3, Pg. 417 (Summarized)*

[46] *al-Kāmil fī al-Tārīkh, 'Inḍimām al-Ḥurr, Vol. 3, Pg. 420 (Summarized)*

29

SAYYIDUNA HURR'S APOLOGY TO THE LOFTY-STATIONED 'IMAM

Ḥurr grudgingly advanced with the unit towards the 'Imām but in such a manner that his body is trembling and those beside him are hearing his heart throbbing in his chest. Witnessing this, someone from his nation said, "This act of yours puts me in suspicion. I have not seen this state of yours in any battle. Whenever someone asks me who is the bravest amongst all the people of *Kūfah*, I only take your name."

He responded, "I am thinking that on one side, the pleasantly colored flowers of Paradise bloom, and on one side, blazing fires of Hell are rising. Even if I am burnt to pieces, I cannot bear to leave Paradise."

He said this, kicked the horse, and presented himself in the service of the Lofty-Stationed 'Imām, Allāh Almighty is pleased with him. He then said, "May Allāh sacrifice me for His Eminence. I am that very companion of His Eminence who prevented His Eminence from returning and who took His Eminence into custody. By Allāh, I had no idea these misfortunate people would not accept His Eminence's command and that they would bring the matter to this. I used to say in my heart, 'Fine. I will do some things as they say so they do not think that I have left their obedience and that at the end, they will at least somewhat accept the command of His Eminence.' By Allāh, if I had any clue that they will not accept anything, then I would not even do this much. I have presented myself after repenting and I wish to sacrifice my life for His Eminence. Will my repentance be accepted according to His Eminence?"

He said, "Yes. Allāh is the acceptor of repentance and forgiver of sins."

Ḥurr heard this glad tiding, turned to his nation, and began to say, "Are those matters presented by the 'Imām not accepted?"

'Ibn Sa`d said, "Accepting them is outside of my jurisdiction."

He said, "O *Kūfīs,* may your mothers be without children. May your mothers be destined your mourning. Did you invite the 'Imām to deliver him to the hands of the enemy? Did you not vow to give your lives for him? And now you are prepared to murder him? You do not even accept that he goes to any city of Allāh wherein he and his family would find safety? You have made him a helpless prisoner? The flowing water of the Euphrates which the enemies of Allāh are drinking and the dogs and swines of the villages are wallowing about in has been withheld from Ḥusayn and his children. The pain of thirst has brought them to the ground. How awfully you have behaved with the offspring of Muḥammad, may Allāh Almighty send blessings and salutations upon him and his progeny. If you do not repent and put an end to your antics, may Allāh keep you thirsty on the Day of Resurrection." [47]

[47] *al-Kāmil fī al-Tārīkh, 'Inḍimām al-Ḥurr, Vol. 3, Pg. 421 (Summarized)*

30

THE BATTLE COMMENCES

In response to this, those malicious people began to pelt stones at Sayyidunā Ḥurr. He retreated and stood in front of the 'Imām.

From the unit of the misfortunate people, Ziyād's slave, Yasār, and 'Ibn Ziyād's slave, Sālim, came to the battlefield and began to request a combatant for their opposition. Sayyidunā `Abd Allāh bin `Umayr Kalbī, Allāh Almighty is pleased with him, came forth. They both said, "We do not know you. Send Zuhayr bin Qayn, Ḥabīb bin Maẓhar, or Barīr bin Ḥuḍayr for our opposition."

Sayyidunā `Abd Allāh said to Yasār, "O son of a sinful mother, will you not battle me? Does your battle require such grand personalities?"

He said this, struck one hand and he was killed. Sālim attacked him and he prevented it with the left hand.

The fingers were blown off. He attacked with the right and he, too, was killed.

This `Abd Allāh presented himself in the service of the 'Imām, Allāh Almighty is pleased with him, from *Kūfah*, and his wife, 'Umm Wahb, was with him. She had taken the pole of the tent and was going for *jihād*. She said to her husband, "May my mother and father be sacrificed for you. Fight for those immaculate, pure offspring of the Prophet!"

He responded, "Go be amongst the women."

She denied and said, "I will die with you."

Finally, the Honorable 'Imām called out and said, "O woman! May Allāh have mercy on you. Go back as *jihād* is not an obligation upon women!" She retreated.

Then, `Amr bin al-Ḥajjāj rode his animal and advanced from the right wing of 'Ibn Sa`d's army. The companions of the 'Imām kneeled and put the spears forward. The horses could not move ahead on the heads of the spears. They turned around and arrows were shot from there. So many of them were wounded and so many killed.

One coward, 'Ibn Ḥawzah, asked, "Is Ḥusayn amongst you?"

No one responded. He asked three times. The people responded, "What do you have to do?"

He said, "O Ḥusayn, glad tidings of the fire to you!"

He responded, "You are a liar. I will go to my Merciful Lord."

He then asked his name. He responded, "'Ibn Ḥawzah."

He then supplicated:

اللهم خذه إلى النار

O Allāh, deliver him to the fire!

Upon hearing this, that outcast became enraged. He moved his horse towards His Eminence. It was the power of Allāh that the horse went berserk, and he fell off. One foot became entangled in the saddle and the horse took off so fast that this outcast's femur and shin were broken, and his skull was broken to pieces after being continuously slammed against rocks. Finally, in this manner, he was sent to Hell.

Masrūq bin Wā'il Ḥaḍramī had come with the intention of taking the Oppressed 'Imām's blessed head. He saw this state of 'Ibn Ḥawzah and began saying, "By Allāh, I will never battle the *'Ahl al-Bayt!*"

Then, Yazīd bin Ma`qil began saying to Sayyidunā Barīr, "What did Allāh do with you?"

He responded, "He did good."

He said, "You have told a lie and I did not know you to be a liar prior to today. I testify that you are misguided."

He said, "Then come. Let us have a *mubāhalah*[48] that Allāh curses the liar and the liar be killed at the hands of the truthful."

He accepted. After the *mubāhalah*, 'Ibn Ma`qil swung his sword to no benefit.

[48] *Mubāhalah: A practice of mutual imprecation to prove the truth of one's point (Translator)*

Sayyidunā Barīr, Allāh Almighty is pleased with him, attacked and tore the brain cutting through the helmet.

Seeing this, Raḍī bin Munqidh `Abdī ran and grappled with Sayyidunā Barīr, Allāh Almighty is pleased with him. They began to wrestle. Sayyidunā Barīr, Allāh Almighty is pleased with him, attacked him and got on his chest. Ka`b bin Jābir 'Azdī struck a spear from behind and it vanished into the blessed back. After being struck with the spear, he got off Raḍī's chest and bit that coward's nose with his teeth. Ka`b swung a sword and he became martyred. When Ka`b turned around, his woman said, "I shall never speak to you! You gave aid to the enemy in the presence of Fāṭimah's son and martyred Barīr, the master of scholars, Allāh Almighty is pleased with him!"[49]

Then came `Amr bin Qaraẓah 'Anṣārī, Allāh Almighty is pleased with him, from the 'Imām's side and was martyred after putting up a severe fight. Sayyidunā Ḥurr battled intensely. Yazīd bin Sufyān came before him, and he killed him. Nāfi` bin Hilāl Murādī, Allāh Almighty is pleased with him, came to the battleground and Muzāḥim bin Ḥarīth became his rival. The content Murādī killed that impotent and misfortunate individual.

Seeing this state, `Amr bin al-Ḥajjāj yelled, "O people! Do you know who you are battling? Before you are those warriors who desire death! Do not battle them one on one! They are very less in number. By Allāh, if you all pelt stones together, you will murder them!"

[49] *al-Kāmil fī al-Tārīkh, al-Ma`rikah, Vol. 3, Pg. 421 (Summarized)*

Preferring this opinion, 'Ibn Sa`d prevented people from solitary battle. Then, `Amr bin al-Ḥajjāj attacked from the side of the Euphrates. From this attack, Muslim bin `Awsajah 'Asadī, Allāh Almighty is pleased with him, received martyrdom.

`Amr retreated and some life remained in him (Sayyidunā Muslim). Ḥabīb bin Maẓhar said, "Glad tidings of Paradise to you. Your falling has become severely difficult for me. I shall meet you very soon. Give me any bequest to carry out."

Muslim, Allāh Almighty is pleased with him, pointed to the Honorable 'Imām and said, "Sacrifice yourself for him."

Ḥabīb responded, "Exactly this shall happen."

Then, the malicious 'Ibn Sa`d sent five hundred archers alongside 'Ibn Numayr to the congregation of the 'Imām.

Now, a shower of arrows begins to pour on those who have been thirsty for three days.

The 'Imām's companions descended from their horses and came on foot.

This coming on foot was done with the wisdom that this unfathomed affliction was coming from five hundred archers at once and the feet must not stagger due to fear.

To kill or be killed, whatever is to happen should happen here. There should be no way to run away abandoning the 'Imām and showing their backs to him.

Sayyidunā Ḥurr battled fiercely to the point that the afternoon came. Those five hundred found no control over his thirty companions.

When the misfortunate 'Ibn Sa`d saw the state that there is no strength to advance from ahead, there were houses to the right and left of the battlefield, he sent men in them so there could be attacks from the right and left as well on the congregation of the 'Imām.

Three or four of the Oppressed 'Imām's companions had already occupied the homes. Whoever jumped in was killed. 'Ibn Sa`d was enraged and said, "Let the houses be set on fire!"

The 'Imām said, "Allow them to burn. When they are burnt, there will remain no danger of an attack from there."[50]

Shimr, the outcast, attacked and moved towards the pure tent. The dweller of Hell asked for fire so he can set the tent of the people of Paradise on fire. His companion, Ḥumayd bin Muslim, said, "Killing women and children by setting the tent on fire is definitely not appropriate."

That dweller of Hell did not accept. Shīth bin Rab`ī Kūfī, who was of the commanders of the impure army, prevented the fire-bound from setting a fire.

Meanwhile, Sayyidunā Zuhayr bin Qayn, alongside ten companions, attacked the outcast Shimr's army with such severity that those misfortunate people were forced to run and show their backs. 'Abū `Uzzah was killed in this attack.

The enemies gathered and surrounded these eleven once again. No matter how many of them (the enemies) were killed, it would go unnoticed due to their plethora, and if any one of these were martyred, it would become apparent to everyone.

It was in this period that the time of *Ẓuhr* arrived. Sayyidunā 'Abū Thumāmah al-Ṣā'idī said to the 'Imām, "My life be sacrificed

[50] *al-Kāmil fī al-Tārīkh, al-Ma`rikah, Vol. 3, Pg. 423 (Summarized)*

for His Eminence. I am seeing that the enemies have now come close. By Allāh, until I give my life for His Eminence, His Eminence will not be martyred. However, I desire that I meet Allāh Almighty having prayed *Ẓuhr*."

The 'Imām responded, "Yes. This is the first portion of the time. Tell them to give us just enough respite that we can pray."

It was a miracle of the 'Imām that this was accepted by those irreligious individuals.

The coward, 'Ibn Numayr, said, "This prayer will not be accepted."

Sayyidunā Ḥabīb bin Maẓhar, Allāh Almighty is pleased with him, responded, "The prayer of the Messenger's family will not be accepted, and O donkey, yours will be accepted?"

He ('Ibn Numayr) attacked him and he (Sayyidunā Ḥabīb) swung his sword. It landed on the horse and the horse fell. Along with it, that outcast also fell to the ground. His companions rushed and carried him away.

He then put up a severe fight. He killed Badīl bin Ṣarīm of *Banū Tamīm* and another *Tamīmī* struck him with a spear. He wanted to get up but the malicious 'Ibn Numayr swung the sword, and he was martyred. May the mercy of Allāh Almighty be upon him. The 'Imām was severely aggrieved by his martyrdom.

Now, Sayyidunā Ḥurr and Zuhayr bin Qayn, Allāh Almighty is pleased with them both, initiate [the plan of] one of them attacking those malicious people and when they become surrounded in the crowd, the other would fight their way forward and free them. When this one would disappear by being surrounded, the first one would attack and come to their rescue.

For a while, this remained the situation. Then, the infantry broke loose on Sayyidunā Ḥurr and martyred him.[51]

It is in *Rawḍah al-Shuhadā'* that when Ḥurr fell wounded, he called out to the 'Imām. His Eminence anxiously went to him and carried him away after putting up a fierce fight. He laid him on the ground, put his head on his own lap, and began wiping the dirt from his forehead and injuries with the lower part of his garment.

Ḥurr opened his eyes, smiled at finding his head in the lap of the 'Imām, and said, "His Eminence is pleased with me now?"

He responded, "We are pleased and may Allāh also be pleased with you."

Ḥurr heard this soul-refreshing glad tiding, gave the treasure of life for the 'Imām, and embarked the path of the lofty Paradise.

آرزو یہ ہے کہ نکلے دم تمہارے سامنے | تم ہمارے سامنے ہو ہم تمہارے سامنے

The desire is that life departs in front of you
You be in front of us, and we be in front of you

صلائے قصہ خواں فرقت کی شب سو یہ کہانی ہے | تیرے زانو ہی کے تکیے پہ مجھ کو نیند آنی ہے

The call of the storyteller on the night of separation was for this story
Sleep shall come to me only on the pillow of your lap

After the martyrdom of Ḥurr, a severe battle commenced. The enemies were continuously slaughtered and kept advancing.

[51] *al-Kāmil fi al-Tārīkh, al-Ma`rikah, Vol. 3, Pg. 425 (Summarized)*

Due to their plethora, they would pay no mind to anything and eventually reached the proximity of the 'Imām. They began pouring a shower of arrows on the thirsty.

Seeing this state, Sayyidunā Ḥanafī [52] took the 'Imām behind his back and stood making his face and chest a shield for the 'Imām. Arrow after arrow is coming from the enemy, but he is taking wounds upon wounds with utter satisfaction and complete pleasure.

At this time, this individual intoxicated by the wine of love has brought back memories of *'Uḥud* by taking his beloved, his adored Ḥusayn, behind his back. There too, a selfless lover stood before the Master of all Beloveds, may Allāh Almighty send blessings and salutations upon him and his progeny, as a shield against the attacks of the enemies when the battle of Muslims deteriorated. This was Sayyidunā Sa`d bin 'Abū Waqāṣ, Allāh Almighty is pleased with him. His Luminous Eminence, may Allāh Almighty send blessings and salutations upon him and his progeny, would stand behind him and continuously grant him arrows from the quiver to dispel the enemies. Upon every arrow, he would say:

ارم سعد بأبي أنت وأمي

Shoot the arrows, O Sa`d! My father and mother be sacrificed for you!

[52] *Sa`īd bin `Abd Allāh Ḥanafī*

The glory of Allāh! In the battle of *'Uḥud*, the selflessness of Sayyidunā Sa`d, Allāh Almighty is pleased with him, was such that he became the shield of Rasūl Allāh, may Allāh Almighty send blessings and salutations upon him and his progeny, and did not allow the enemy to get close. In the occurrence of *Karbalā*, the ill will of 'Ibn Sa`d was such that he has brought the enemies to the opposition of the son of Allāh's Messenger, may Allāh Almighty send blessings and salutations upon him and his progeny. The honorable father's arrows were being shot at the enemies of *'Islām* and the misguided son's arrows are being shot at the master of Muslims.

ببیں تفاوت رہ کجاست تا کجا

See how far apart the difference of paths is!

In short, Sayyidunā Ḥanafī was wounded by arrows in front of the 'Imām, Allāh Almighty is pleased with him, to the point that he became a martyr and fell. May the mercy of Allāh Almighty be upon him.

Sayyidunā Zuhayr bin Qayn, Allāh Almighty is pleased with him, put up an extremely diligent effort to put an end to this storm of disrespect and was martyred after putting up a severe fight.

Sayyidunā Nāfi` bin Hilāl, Allāh Almighty is pleased with him, had his name engraved on arrows and soaked them in poison. Twelve misfortunate people were killed by them and countless were wounded.

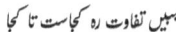

The enemies eventually surrounded him too and because of both of his arms being broken, he was forcefully taken captive. The malicious Shimr took him to 'Ibn Sa`d.

The moonlike face of Hilāl was covered in blood and that courageous lion was saying, "I made twelve of you fall and wounded an uncountable number. Had my arms not broken, I would not have been taken captive."

Shimr unsheathed his sword for his murder, and he (Hilāl) said, "Had you been Muslim, by Allāh, you would not prefer to meet Allāh having shed our blood! Praise be to Allāh, the One who kept our death at the hands of the worst of creation."

Shimr martyred him and then began attacking the remainder of Muslims. The 'Imām's companions saw that they no longer had the strength to protect the 'Imām. They began to rush towards martyrdom lest any harm reaches the *`Arsh*-Stationed 'Imām while they remain alive.

Sayyidunā `Abd Allāh and `Abd al-Raḥmān, the sons of `Urwah Ghifārī, sought permission, advanced, and were martyred after involving themselves in battle.

Sayf bin Ḥārith and Mālik bin `Abd, Allāh Almighty is pleased with them both, two sons of one mother and cousins from their fathers' side, presented themselves in service and began to cry. The 'Imām said, "Why do you cry? Only a brief period remains until Allāh Almighty cools your eyes."

They responded, "By Allāh, we do not cry for ourselves, but we cry for His Eminence as we now lack the strength to defend His Eminence."

He said, "May Allāh reward you."

Thereafter, both of them also took leave, advanced, and were martyred.

Ḥanẓalah bin 'As`ad, Allāh Almighty is pleased with him, recited a few verses of the Glorious *Qur'ān* in front of the 'Imām and attempted to instill fear of Allāh's torment into the *Kūfīs*, but who would heed to such on that side?

He too took leave after saying *salām* and became a martyr after a display of great courage.

Shawdhab bin Shākir, Allāh Almighty is pleased with him, advanced after taking leave and reached the Abode of Peace following the receipt of martyrdom.

Sayyidunā `Ābis, Allāh Almighty is pleased with him, took permission and departed. He sought a rival, but no one stepped forward fearing his renowned bravery. 'Ibn Sa`d said, "Pelt him with stones!"

A shower of stones commenced from all four directions. When he saw this antic of these cowards, he became full of rage. Taking off his armor and throwing his helmet, he attacked, and in just a moment's time, he made everyone flee. The enemy then came after gathering their senses and martyred him too. Yazīd bin 'Abū Ziyād Kindī, Allāh Almighty is pleased with him, who was previously a part of the *Kūfī* army and came to the light leaving the fire, started shooting arrows at the enemies. Upon his every arrow, the 'Imām supplicated, "O Allāh, may his arrow not miss and grant him Paradise!"

He shot one hundred arrows of which not even five went amiss. Ultimately, he was martyred.

In this occurrence, he was the first to attain martyrdom and the chronological list of the martyrs of *Karbalā* commences with his very name. `Amr bin Khālid, alongside Sa`d Mawlā, Jabbār bin Ḥārith, and Majma` bin `Ubayd Allāh, Allāh Almighty is pleased with them, fought until they drowned amongst the enemies. At this time, the enemies had attacked fiercely. Sayyidunā `Abbās, Allāh Almighty is pleased with him, attacked and rescued them. He was shredded by wounds, but he broke loose on the enemies in this very state. After continuously fighting, he was martyred.

31

THE MARTYRDOM OF FLOWERS FROM THE PROPHETIC GARDEN COMMENCES

At this time, there did not remain amongst the loyal and selfless soldiers of the 'Imām, save a few relatives. The first of these honorable individuals to step towards the battle of the enemies was the 'Imām's son, Sayyidunā `Alī 'Akbar [53], Allāh Almighty is pleased with him.

The attack of a lion is well-known and this lion, after all, is a lion from the Muḥammadan den. May Allāh protect from its enraged attack! He displayed a sample of Allāh's wrath to the enemies. Whoever lifted their head was lowered.

[53] *His noble mother was Sayyidah Laylā bint 'Abū Murrah and not Sayyidah Shahr Bānū as is widespread amongst the general masses.*

Wherever he advanced with line-disturbing attacks, the enemy would disperse like moss. He battled for long and killed continuously.

The thirst intensified even further. He retreated, and after catching his breath, he attacked again and raised the same doomsday on the life of the enemies. The same happened a few times until the spear of the doomed Murrah bin Munqidh `Abdī struck and the ill-fated put him on the swords. He took his rest in the lofty Paradise.

Upon his young son's body, the 'Imām said, "O son, may Allāh kill those who martyred you. After you, there is not but soil on the earth. How audacious before Allāh is this nation, and how daring they are in the dishonoring of the Messenger, may Allāh Almighty send blessings and salutations upon him and his progeny."

He then lifted the blessed corpse and placed it by the tent.

Thereafter, `Abd Allāh bin Muslim advanced to battle and was martyred.[54]

Now, the enemies swarmed in from all four directions. In this mob, `Awn bin `Abd Allāh bin Sayyidunā Ja`far Ṭayyār and the sons of `Aqīl, `Abd al-Raḥmān and Ja`far, attained martyrdom.

Then, Sayyidunā Qāsim, the son of Sayyidunā 'Imām Ḥasan, Allāh Almighty is pleased with him, attacked and fell to the ground after being struck by the sword of the outcast, `Amr bin Sa`d bin Nufayl. He called out to the 'Imām saying, "Uncle!"

The 'Imām arrived like an enraged lion and let his sword loose on the outcast, `Amr. He tried to prevent it and his arm was

[54] *al-Kāmil fī al-Tārīkh, wa Kāna 'Awwal Man Qutila, Vol. 3, Pg. 428 (Summarized)*

blown off by the elbow. He yelled and the cavalry of *Kūfah* rushed to his aid. Amongst the sand and soil, the stampede of the horses landed on his own impure chest. When the cloud of sand cleared, it was seen that the 'Imām is saying to the corpse of Sayyidunā Qāsim, "O Qāsim, your murderers are distant from the mercy of Allāh! By Allāh, it heavily burdens your uncle that you called him, and he was unable to arrive at your cry for aid."

He then lifted him to his chest as well and carried him away. He laid him down besides Sayyidunā `Alī 'Akbar.

In this same manner, one after another, Sayyidunā `Abbās, all three of his brothers, another one of the 'Imām's sons, Sayyidunā 'Abū Bakr, and all the brothers and nephews, Allāh Almighty is pleased with them, were martyred. May Allāh grant them abode in His vast forms of mercy and benefit us by their blessings.

At this time, the Oppressed 'Imām is left alone. He goes to the tent and comes to the battlefield with his youngest son, Sayyidunā `Abd Allāh (who is commonly known as `Alī 'Aṣghar amongst the general masses), in his arms. One ill-fated individual shot an arrow, and he was slaughtered in those very arms. The 'Imām allowed his blood to flow to the ground and supplicated, "O Allāh, if you have barred celestial aid from us, grant a good outcome and take revenge from these oppressors."[55]

[55] *al-Kāmil fī al-Tārīkh, wa Kāna 'Awwal Man Qutila, Vol. 3, Pg. 429 (Summarized)*

پھول کھل کھل کر بہاریں اپنی سب دکھلا گئے | حسرت ان غنچوں پر ہے جو بے کھلے مرجھا گئے

Flowers have all shown their blossoming after having grown
Astonishment is at those buds that wilted without growing

اللهم صل على سيدنا ومولانا محمد وعلى اٰله وأصحابه أجمعين

O Allāh send blessings upon our master and chief, Muḥammad, and upon all of his offspring and companions.

32

THE MARTYRDOM OF THE LOFTY-STATIONED ʿIMAM

رضي الله عنه

Those familiar with the commonalities of beauty and love recognize that the union of the beloved, which the lover holds dearer than his own life, is not attained without taking on afflictions and enduring hardships.

اے دل بہوس بر سر کارے نرسی　　تا غم نہ خوری بغم گسارے نرسی

O heart, you shall not reach felicity by greed
You will not have reach to the consoler until you have tasted sorrow

تا سوده نہ گردی چو حنا در تہ سنگ | ہرگز بکف پائے نگارے نرسی

Until you have been ground beneath a stone like henna
You will not be able to have reach to the sole [of the foot] of the beloved

The heart is pierced with a dagger and broken. Knives are stabbed into the liver and abandoned.

Then, emphasis is given on the fact that the name will be crossed off the register of lovers if one should utter even a groan.

In other words, they ascertain beforehand and test [the lovers]. Then, at some point, arises the opportunity of giving a single glimpse from the veil.

خوباں دل و جاں بینوا میخواہند | زخمے کہ زنند مرحبا میخواہند

The beloved seeks such hearts and lives from the lovers which are soundless
They will deliver wounds and expect welcoming from those same people

ایں قوم ایں قوم چشم بد دور ایں قوم | خون می ریزند و خوں بہا میخواہند

This group, may the evil eye be repelled from them, is an astonishing group
They shed blood themselves and then demand blood-money

Furthermore, this examination is not only the tradition of a few beauts of the era.

This is even the tradition of the alluring manifestations and the fascinating displays of the Ever-Present Beauty as it is said:

وَلَنَبْلُوَنَّكُم بِشَيْءٍ مِّنَ الْخَوْفِ وَالْجُوعِ وَنَقْصٍ مِّنَ الْأَمْوَالِ وَالْأَنفُسِ وَالثَّمَرَاتِ

And We shall surely examine you all with something of fear, hunger, deficiency of wealth, lives, and fruits.[56]

When those times have been tolerated and those afflictions have been endured, then what is to be asked? The royal curtain of beauty is lifted from the yearning eyes and the heart anxious for eras is made an embodiment of peace and tranquility.

This is the very basis upon which the Oppressed 'Imām, Allāh Almighty is pleased with him, has been taken away from his homeland and has been brought as a foreigner to the plain of *Karbalā*. Moreover, from this morning, he has been separated from his companions, comrades, and even those brought up in his arms, one by one. Pieces of his heart lay before his eyes bathed in blood. Pleasant and delicate flowers of a green and prolific garden have been mixed into the earth after being torn to petals, yet there is no concern. If there was any concern, then why should there be? As this is the day for which those who gave up their homes in the path of the Beloved had departed from *Madīnah*. That is why each had been sent and was sacrificed. Those who could not come on their own feet, he brought them in his arms and offered them.

Where are those Angels who questioned the birth of the honorable humankind? They should rise from their prayer-mats

[56] *Sūrah al-Baqarah, 155*

and their *muṣallās* of *taṣbīḥ* (glorification) and *taqdīs* (sanctification) and journey to the plain of *Karbalā* today. They will witness, with a gaze of astonishment, a magnificent elucidation of:

إِنِّيٓ أَعۡلَمُ مَا لَا تَعۡلَمُونَ

Indeed, I know what you all do not know.[57]

In this heart-wrenching battle, the test of everyone was intended, but that of the Oppressed Ḥusayn was essential, and that of the others was secondary. If this was not so, it would be possible that the 'Imām would be martyred first at the hands of those enemies who were only an enemy to the 'Imām and thirsty for the blood of the 'Imām alone.

Allāhu 'Akbar! What a painful view of a doomsday was before the eyes. The Oppressed 'Imām is parting from his household. In a position of helplessness, a state of loneliness, parched for three days, having taken hundreds of arrows to the sacred heart, he is preparing to go to battle against the thousands of enemies.

The young daughters of the *'Ahl al-Bayt*, regarding whose pampering in the world the final decision will be made alongside his martyrdom, are crying out of anxiety. Helpless chieftesses, the conclusion of whose luxury and whose peace will say farewell alongside his departure, are in tears with severe distress.

A few sanctified figures, whom to call talking images of helplessness would be appropriate in every way, whose wifehood

[57] *Sūrah al-Baqarah: 30 (Translation of verse added by translator)*

was to be mixed in with the dirt, and whose hopes would break along with his sacred breath, have become crushed after continuous crying. Along with the stillness and silence on their pale faces, the chain of continuous and uninterrupted tears gives constant glimpses of the condition and says:

می روی و گریہ می آید مرا | ساعتے بنشیں کہ باراں بگزرد

Your departure makes me cry
Sit for a while so that I may find peace and my tears stop

At this time, someone ask the heart of Sayyidunā 'Imām Zayn al-`Ābidīn, Allāh Almighty is pleased with him, what kinds of heartaches the fragile heart of His Eminence endured on this day and to tolerate what kind of an affliction are preparations being made. What state have illness, a foreign land, the separation of companions from childhood, the estrangement of his playmates, and the scar of his beloved brothers made of the heart? Now even the shade of the one who catered to his demands, the merciful father who pampered him, will soon be lifted from over the blessed head. What is strange in this is that in these afflictions and these unbearable hardships, there is no one to even express concern.

درد دل اٹھ اٹھ کے کس کا راستہ تکتا ہے تو | پوچھنے والا مریض بے کسی کا کون ہے

Throbbing of the heart, whose path do you continuously rise to see?
Who is there to ask about the patient of helplessness?

Now, the 'Imām, Allāh Almighty is pleased with him, has left after embracing the children, bidding patience unto the women, and having granted his final viewing.

از پیش من آں رشک چمن میگزرد | چوں روح روانیکہ زتن میگزرد

The beloved, who is the envy of the garden, vanishes from my gaze
Like the soul departs from the body

حال عجبے روز وداعش دارم | من از سر و جاں از من میگزرد

Upon his departure, my state is strange
It is as though I am separating from the head and life is separating from me

Alas! At this time, there is not even someone who will hold the saddle to ascend him on horseback or accompany him to the battlefield.

However, there are the painful cries of helpless children and gazes full of despair of powerless women that are with the 'Imām at every single step.

With every step of the Oppressed 'Imām that moves forward, orphanhood moves closer to the children, and helplessness to the women.

The associates of the 'Imām, the sisters of the 'Imām who were just given instruction of patience, sit in a state of silence having placed a heavy slab of patience over their wounded hearts.

However, the uninterrupted chain of their tears and the paling of their faces overwhelmed by helplessness, upon the martyrdom of their loved ones, the departure of the 'Imām, Allāh Almighty is pleased with him, their own powerlessness, and the destruction of their household, is saying by way of expression:

مجھ کو جنگل میں اکیلا چھوڑ کر　　　قافلہ سارا روانہ ہو گیا

Leaving me alone in the jungle
The caravan's entirety has departed

33

THE LATTER PART OF HISTORY AND THE MARTYRDOM OF THE PARCHED 'IMAM

باغ جنت کے ہیں بہرِ مدح خوان اِہلبیت
تم کو مژدہ نار کا اے دشمنانِ اہلبیت

The gardens of Heaven are for the one who praises the 'Ahl al-Bayt
Tidings of the fire to you, O foes of the 'Ahl al-Bayt!

کس زباں سے ہو بیانِ عز و شانِ اہلبیت
مدح گوئے مصطفی ہے مدح خوانِ اہلبیت

By which tongue can be said the honor and grandeur of the 'Ahl al-Bayt?
He who praises Muṣṭafā is the One who praises the 'Ahl al-Bayt

ان کی پاکی کا خدائے پاک کرتا ہے بیاں
آیۂ تطہیر سے ظاہر ہے شانِ اہلبیت

The Pure Deity mentions the purity of theirs
By the verse of Taṭhīr is manifest, the grandeur of the 'Ahl al-Bayt

مصطفٰی عزت بڑھانے کے لیے تعظیم دیں
ہے بلند اقبال تیرا دودمانِ اہلبیت

Muṣṭafā gives honor to elevate the reverence
Lofty is your eminence, O dynasty of the 'Ahl al-Bayt!

ان کے گھر میں بے اجازت جبریل آتے نہیں
قدر والے جانتے ہیں قدر و شانِ اہلبیت

In their home without permission, Jibrīl does not enter
Those of stature recognize the stature and grandeur of the 'Ahl al-Bayt

مصطفٰی بائع خریدار اس کا اللہ اشتری
خوب چاندی کر رہا ہے کاروانِ اہلبیت

Muṣṭafā its seller, and its purchaser? Allāh is purchasing!
Becoming very prosperous is the caravan of the 'Ahl al-Bayt

رزم کا میدان بنا ہے جلوہ گاہِ حسن و عشق
کربلا میں ہو رہا ہے امتحانِ اہلبیت

The battlefield has become a station of manifesting beauty and love
In Karbalā is transpiring, a test of the 'Ahl al-Bayt

پھول زخموں کے کھلائے ہیں ہوائے دوست نے

خون سے سینچا گیا ہے گلستانِ اہلبیت

The friendly winds have blossomed flowers of wounds
Watered by blood is the garden of the 'Ahl al-Bayt

حوریں کرتی ہے عروسانِ شہادت کا سنگار

خوبرو دولھا بنا ہے ہر جوانِ اہلبیت

Ḥūrs adorn themselves for the grooms of martyrdom
Have become a handsome groom, all the youth of the 'Ahl al-Bayt

ہو گئی تحقیقِ عید، دیدِ آبِ تیغ سے

اپنے روزے کھولتے ہیں صائمانِ اہلبیت

The festival has become ascertained by the vision of the sword's edge
Open their fasts, the fasters of the 'Ahl al-Bayt

جمعہ کا دن ہے کتابیں زیست کی طے کر کے آج

کھیلتے ہیں جان پر شہزادگانِ اہلبیت

'Tis the day of Jumu`ah – today, after folding the books of life
Play on life, the princes of the 'Ahl al-Bayt

اے شبابِ فصلِ گل یہ چل گئی کیسی ہوا

کٹ رہا ہے لہلہاتا بوستانِ اہلبیت

O youth of the season of flowers, what kind of wind has blown?
Being chopped is the swaying garden of the 'Ahl al-Bayt

کس شقی کی ہے حکومت ہائے کیا اندھیر ہے
دن دھاڑے لٹ رہا ہے کاروانِ اہلبیت

Which ill-fated individual's rule is it? Alas, how dark it is!
Being robbed in broad daylight is the caravan of the 'Ahl al-Bayt

خشک ہو جا خاک ہو کر خاک میں مل جا فرات
خاک تجھ پر دیکھ تو سوکھی زبانِ اہلبیت

Become dried up after turning to dust – mix into the dirt O Euphrates!
Dirt be upon you, look at the dried tongue of the 'Ahl al-Bayt

خاک پر عباس و عثمانِ علمبردار ہیں
بیکسی اب کون اٹھائے گا نشانِ اہلبیت

On the soil are the flagbearers, \`Abbās and \`Uthmān
Helplessness – who will now raise the symbol of the 'Ahl al-Bayt?

تیری قدرت جانور تک آب سے سیراب ہوں
پیاس کی شدت میں تڑپے بے زبانِ اہلبیت

Your power! Even the animals are quenched by water
Suffer in the intensity of thirst, the tongueless of the 'Ahl al-Bayt

قافلہ سالار منزل کو چلے ہیں سونپ کر
وارثِ بے وارثاں کو کاروانِ اہلبیت

The caravan leader advances to the destination after entrusting
To the One who survives all and has no heirs, the caravan of the 'Ahl al-Bayt

فاطمہ کے لاڈلے کا آخری دیدار ہے

حشر کا ہنگامہ برپا ہے میانِ اہلبیت

'Tis the final viewing of Fāṭimah's dear child
Commotion of Doomsday has broken loose amongst the 'Ahl al-Bayt

وقتِ رخصت کہہ رہا ہے خاک میں ملتا سہاگ

لو سلامِ آخری اے بیوگانِ اہلبیت

At the time of departure, the wifehood mixing in with the dirt is saying
Take the final salām, O widower of the 'Ahl al-Bayt

ابرِ فوجِ دشمناں میں اے فلک یوں ڈوب جائے

فاطمہ کا چاند مہرِ آسمانِ اہلبیت

In a cloud of enemy forces, O sky, drowns in such a manner
The moon of Fāṭimah, the sun of the sky of the 'Ahl al-Bayt

کس مزے کی لذتیں ہیں آبِ تیغِ یار میں

خاک و خوں میں لوٹتے ہیں تشنگانِ اہلبیت

The pleasures of which amusement are in the edge of the friend's sword?
In soil and blood tumble the thirsty of the 'Ahl al-Bayt

باغِ جنت چھوڑ کر آئے ہیں محبوبِ خدا

اے زہے قسمت تمہاری کشتگانِ اہلبیت

Leaving the garden of Paradise, the Beloved of Allāh has come
Oh, your good fortune, slain of the 'Ahl al-Bayt

حوریں بے پردہ نکل آئی ہیں سر کھولے ہوئے

آج کیسا حشر ہے یا رب میانِ اہلبیت

The Ḥūrs have come out unveiled, having revealed their heads
What kind of a doomsday is today, O Lord, amongst the 'Ahl al-Bayt

کوئی کیوں پوچھے کسی کو کیا غرض اے بیکسی

آج کیسا ہے مریض نیم جانِ اہلبیت

Why shall anyone ask? Who has any care? Oh hopelessness!
How is, on this day, the life-lacking patient of the 'Ahl al-Bayt?

گھر لٹانا جان دینا کوئی تجھ سے سیکھ جائے

جانِ عالم ہو فدا اے خاندانِ اہلبیت

Sacrificing the home, giving life, one shall learn from you
May the life of the universe be your ransom O family of the 'Ahl al-Bayt

سر شہیدانِ محبت کے ہیں نیزوں پر بلند

اور اونچی کی خدا نے قدر و شانِ اہلبیت

The heads of the martyrs of love are raised on spears
Allāh exalted even more the stature and grandeur of the 'Ahl al-Bayt

دولتِ دیدار پائی پاک جانیں بیچ کر

کربلا میں خوب ہی چمکی دوکانِ اہلبیت

They attained the treasure of vision after selling pure lives
In Karbalā, marvelously shined, the shop of the 'Ahl al-Bayt

زخم کھانے کو تو آبِ تیغ پینے کو دیا
خوب دعوت کی بلا کر دشمنانِ اہلبیت

Wounds given to eat and the edge of the sword to drink
Grandly you hosted a feast after inviting, enemies of the 'Ahl al-Bayt

اپنا سودا بیچ کر بازار سونا کر گئے
کونسی بستی بسائی تاجرانِ اہلبیت

You left the market deserted after selling your goods
Which village have you settled in, tradesmen of the 'Ahl al-Bayt?

اہلِ بیتِ پاک سے گستاخیاں بے باکیاں
لعنۃ اللہ علیکم دشمنانِ اہلبیت

Blasphemy and contempt in the court of the pure 'Ahl al-Bayt?
The curse of Allāh be upon you, O foes of the 'Ahl al-Bayt

بے ادب گستاخ فرقے کو سنا دے اے حسنؔ
یوں کہا کرتے ہیں سنی داستانِ اہلبیت

Let the disrespectful, blasphemous sect hear it, O Ḥasan
In this way a Sunnī tells the story of the 'Ahl al-Bayt

O *Kawthar*! Prepare a distribution point of your cold and pleasant water as those thirsty for three days will appear at your riverbed!

O *Ṭūbā*! Extend your shade even further! Those who laid in the sun of *Karbalā* will seek rest beneath you!

Today, *Ḥūrs* from the Heavens have presented themselves in the plain of *Karbalā* having beautified themselves and bearing vessels of cold water. The continuous arrival of Angels from the sky have fully occupied the canopy of the atmosphere and the pure souls have deserted the homes of Paradise. His Luminous Eminence, may Allāh Almighty send blessings and salutations upon him and his progeny, himself has come from *Madīnah Ṭayyibah* to his dear son Ḥusayn's murder ground.

The hair of the blessed beard and the pure head is enveloped in dust, and a chain of tears is tied to the eye. In the blessed hand is a vial in which the blood of the martyrs has been collected. Now comes the time to insert the blood of the sanctified heart's peace, the beloved Ḥusayn.

بچہ ناز رفتہ باشد ز جہاں نیاز مندے | کہ بوقت جان سپردن برسرش رسیدہ باشی

Your admirer must have departed from the world with such pride and fashion
When you would have been present at his side at the time of life's surrender

In short, there was a *Ḥusaynī* festival transpiring in *Karbalā* on this day.

Tell the *Ḥūrs* to untie their fragrant braids and cleanse the plain of *Karbalā* as the time for the son of your princess, your bountiful chieftess, Fāṭimah Zahrā, Allāh Almighty is pleased with her, to be martyred and laid on the soil grows closer.

Inform Riḍwān to adorn the Heavens with pleasant fragrances, embellish it with appealing ornaments, and prepare it as a bride because the groom of martyrdom's gathering is soon to arrive having tied a turban of flowing blood and wearing a garland of wounds around his neck.

ساعت آہ و بکا و بے قراری آ گئی | سید مظلوم کی رن میں سواری آ گئی

The hour of weeping, crying, and anxiety has come
The transportation has arrived in the battlefield of the oppressed master

ساتھ والے بھائی بیٹے ہو چکے ہیں سب شہید | اب امام بے کس و تنہا کی باری آ گئی

The accompanying brothers and sons have all become martyrs
Now, the turn of the helpless and lone 'Imām has arrived

The 'Imām saw the malicious Shimr advancing towards the pure tent and said, "Woe to you! If you do not have a religion and do not fear Doomsday, then at least do not abandon civility! Keep your ignorant transgressors away from my *'Ahl al-Bayt*! The enemy must stay away from there!"

At this time, the Oppressed 'Imām, who has been brought to solitude against thousands of enemies by the desire of martyrdom, is surrounded by all four directions. If the 'Imām attacks to the right side, there remains no sign of the cavalry nor the infantry in the distance. If he goes to the left side, the enemy is forced to run away abandoning the battlefield.

By Allāh, that army would dread these attacks of his like a lion coming to the neck of goats. The battle is prolonged. The enemies have lost their wits. Unexpectedly, the 'Imām's horse became worn out. He battled in such a manner on foot that would not be possible by those on horseback.

He was thirsty for three days and one misfortunate individual pointed towards the Euphrates and said, "Look how it glistens! However, you will not receive so much as a drop from it such that you will be killed thirsty!"

He responded, "May Allāh kill you in a state of thirst!"

Immediately, he began to suffer from thirst. He would drink water, but the thirst would fail to be quenched such that he perished in that very state of thirst.

He would attack and say, "Have you gathered for my killing? Yes, yes. By Allāh, you will not kill anyone after me whose killing will be more of a means for the displeasure of Allāh than my killing. By Allāh, I anticipate that Allāh Almighty will grant me honor by your dishonor. He will take such revenge from you that will not even be in your imagination or dreams. By Allāh, if you murder me, He will sow the seed of discord amongst you and shed your blood! He will not be pleased at just this much such that He increases painful torment for you little by little!"[58]

When the malicious Shimr did not see the task being accomplished, he taunted the army, "May your mothers beat you! What are you waiting for? Kill Ḥusayn!"

Now, from all four directions, billows of darkness and clouds of blackness overcast the moon of Fāṭimah, Allāh Almighty is pleased with her.

Zur`ah bin Sharīk Tamīmī struck a sword on the blessed left shoulder. The 'Imām has become exhausted. He is torn by wounds.

[58] *al-Kāmil fī al-Tārīkh, al-Ma`rikah, Vol. 3, Pg. 431*

He bears thirty-three spear wounds and thirty-four gashes of swords. There is no count of how many are that of arrows. He wills to get up and falls. In this very state, Sinān bin 'Anas Nakha`ī, the ill-fated dweller of the fire and Hell-bound, strikes a spear and that star of the *`Arsh* shoots and falls to the ground.

The outcast Sinān says to Khawlī bin Yazīd, "Decapitate him."

His hand trembled and Sinān, the offspring of Shayṭān, said, "May your hand go to waste."

He descended from the horse himself and slaughtered and removed the blessed head of the piece of Muḥammad Rasūl Allāh's, may Allāh Almighty send blessings and salutations upon him and his progeny, heart, the one thirsty for three days.

Martyrdom, which sat awaiting this very moment as a bride adorned in a red dress and heavenly fragrances, excitedly runs after lifting its veil and embraces its groom, Ḥusayn the Martyr, Allāh Almighty is pleased with him, wrapping its arms around his neck.

فصلى الله على سيدنا ومولانا محمد وآله وصحبه أجمعين

ولعنة الله على أعدائه وأعدائهم الظّٰلمين

May Allāh send blessings upon our master and our chief, Muḥammad, and all of his progeny and companions. May the curse of Allāh be upon his enemies and their enemies, the oppressors.

They did not find solace on even this. They stripped the blessed attire of the 'Imām and distributed it amongst themselves. The fire of animosity was still not extinguished.

They looted the tents of the *'Ahl al-Bayt*, all the wealth and luggage. They removed the jewelry of Muḥammad Rasūl Allāh's, may Allāh Almighty send blessings and salutations upon him and his progeny, princesses. They did not leave even an earring on the ear of any woman.

Thousands of the curses of Allāh, the One, the Subduer, on the ill fate of these heathens. Jewelry aside, even the scarves from the heads of the *'Ahl al-Bayt* [were snatched]!

Even then, these outcasts failed to find peace. One ill-fated dweller of the fire and Hell-bound announced, "Is there anyone to trample the body of Ḥusayn with horses?"

Ten outcasts galloped their horses and trampled with carriages the blessed chest of the one brought up in the lap of Fāṭimah, Allāh Almighty is pleased with her, and the one who played on the chest of Muṣṭafā, may Allāh Almighty send blessings and salutations upon him and his progeny, to the point that all of the bones of the chest and graceful back shattered to pieces.[59]

صلی اللہ علی سیدنا ومولانا محمد وآلہ وصحبہ أجمعین

ولعنۃ اللہ علی أعدائہ وأعدائھم الظّٰلمین

May Allāh send blessings upon our master and our chief, Muḥammad, and all of his progeny and companions. May the curse of Allāh be upon his enemies and their enemies, the oppressors.

[59] *al-Kāmil fī al-Tārīkh, al-Maʿrikah, Vol. 3, Pg. 432*

34

OCCURRENCES FOLLOWING THE MARTYRDOM

The twisted hound, the malicious Shimr, wanted to martyr 'Imām Zayn al-`Abdīn, Allāh Almighty is pleased with him, as well. Ḥumayd bin Muslim said, "Glory be to Allāh! Will children be killed too?"

The oppressor restrained himself.[60]

Afterwards, the blessed head of the Oppressed 'Imām and that of the martyrs enveloped in mercy were sent to 'Ibn Ziyād with Khawlī bin Yazīd and Ḥumayd bin Muslim. When they reached *Kūfah*, they found his house to be closed. Khawlī brought the blessed head to his house and said to his wife Nawār, "I have brought for you that which will make one wealthy for a lifetime."

She asked, "What is it?"

[60] *al-Kāmil fī al-Tārīkh, al-Ma`rikah, Vol. 3, Pg. 433 and others*

He responded, "The head of Ḥusayn."

She said, "Woe to you! People bring silver and gold and you have brought the head of Rasūl Allāh's, may Allāh Almighty send blessings and salutations upon him and his progeny, son? By Allāh, I shall never live with you!"

This lady says, "Throughout the entire night, I saw a brilliant light had risen from the blessed head to the sky and white birds are sacrificing themselves for the sanctified head."[61]

When the blessed head was brought to the malicious 'Ibn Ziyād, blood began to flow from the door and walls of his house. That ill-fated individual touched the blessed teeth with a staff and said, "I have never seen someone so beautiful. How wonderful are the teeth."

Zayd bin 'Arqam, Allāh Almighty be pleased with him, was seated there, he said, "Move your staff! For ages I have witnessed the Messenger of Allāh, may Allāh Almighty send blessings and salutations upon him and his progeny, kissing these very lips and showing love to them!"

He said this and began to cry.

That malicious individual responded, "May crying be your fate. Had you not gone senile, I would have decapitated you."

He got up to stand and said to the courtiers of this outcast, "You murdered the son, Allāh Almighty is pleased with him, of Fāṭimah and appointed the child of Marjānah as a leader. Today onwards, you are slaves! By Allāh, those dearest to you shall be slain and those who are saved will be made slaves! Those pleased

[61] *al-Kāmil fī al-Tārīkh, al-Ma`rikah, Vol. 3, Pg. 434 and others*

with disgrace and humiliation get away!" He then said, "O 'Ibn Ziyād! I will surely narrate the *ḥadīth* to you that will throw you to the fire of wrath and rage! I saw His Sanctified Eminence, may Allāh Almighty send blessings and salutations upon him, seat Ḥasan on the right thigh and Ḥusayn on the left, place the sanctified hand on their heads, and supplicate, 'My Lord! I entrust these two to You and to the righteous Muslims!' O 'Ibn Ziyād, look at what you have done with the trust of the Prophet, may Allāh Almighty send blessings and salutations upon him and his progeny!"

Elsewhere, the oppressors had put a leash around the neck of the ill `Ābid and cuffs around his hands, and the women were put on camels and were made to depart from *Karbalā* two days later.

سوار گھوڑوں پر أعداء پیادہ شہزادہ | الٰہی کیسا زمانے نے انقلاب کیا

The enemies riding on horses and the prince on foot
O Allāh, how times have changed

When this caravan of looted victims of oppression passed over the corpses of the martyrs that lay in the plain without a grave or shroud, Lady Zaynab, Allāh Almighty be pleased with her, frantically called out, "O Messenger of Allāh! *Ṣalawāt* from the Angels of the sky be on His Eminence! Your Eminence! This is Ḥusayn! He lays in the plain! From head to toe he is covered in blood! The joints of his entire body have been cut! The daughters of His Eminence have been taken captive, and the children of His

Eminence lay killed upon whom the wind blows dust over." [62]

When this oppressed caravan reached the malicious 'Ibn Ziyād, he argued with the oppressed `Ābid and astounded upon receiving a silencing response, he said, "By Allāh, you are one of them yourself!"

Thereafter, he said to another individual, "Check whether he is mature."

Upon this, Murrī bin Mu`ādh 'Aḥmarī, the ill-fated, unclothed the oppressed master, Allāh Almighty is pleased with him, saw, and said, "Yes. He is pubescent."

The malicious individual responded, "Kill him too."

Lady Zaynab, Allāh Almighty is pleased with her, frantically embraced her oppressed nephew and said, "'Ibn Ziyād that is enough! Have you still not become satisfied by our blood? Who have you left amongst us? I bid you the sake of Allāh! If you kill this child, then kill me alongside him!"

The oppressed `Ābid, Allāh Almighty is pleased with him, said, "O 'Ibn Ziyād! Who will remain as the supervisor of these helpless women? You have destroyed your religion, integrity, and the rights of the Messenger. After all, you have some relation to them. Bearing this much in mind, appoint a pious person with them who can take them to *Madīnah* with 'Islāmic etiquettes."

Seeing this state of Lady Zaynab, Allāh Almighty is pleased with her, the malicious individual said, "What a thing the relation of blood is. I truly believe that this woman wants that if I

[62] *al-Kāmil fī al-Tārīkh, al-Ma`rikah, Vol. 3, Pg. 434*

kill this boy, I kill her as well. Well then, I will leave the boy to live with his honor."[63]

[63] *al-Kāmil fī al-Tārīkh, al-Ma`rikah, Vol. 3, Pg. 435*

35

MIRACLES OF THE LUMINOUS HEAD

At this time, this caravan and the heads of the martyrs have been made to depart to Greater Syria (*Shām*). The blessed head was on a spear and along the way, someone was reciting the Glorious *Qur'ān*.

When he reached the verse:

أَمْ حَسِبْتَ أَنَّ أَصْحَابَ الْكَهْفِ وَالرَّقِيمِ كَانُوا مِنْ آيَاتِنَا عَجَبًا

Did you consider that the ones of Kahf and Raqīm were of Our marvelous signs?[64]

[64] *The Glorious Qur'ān, Sūrah al-Kahf: 9*

The blessed head responded:

يا تالی القرءان أعجب من قصة أصحاب الكهف قتلی وحملی

O reciter of the Qur'ān! More astonishing than the story of the people of Kahf is my murdering and being carried [on a spear].

Wherever the oppressors would halt, they would place the blessed head on a spear and guard it.[65]

One Christian priest saw and asked, so he was told. He said, "You are evil people. Will you take ten thousand *'ashrafis* and be okay with this head staying with me for one night?"

The hounds of the world accepted.

The priest took the blessed head, bathed it, applied fragrance to it, and keeping it on his thigh, he continuously saw a light rising from it all throughout the night. The priest spent this night in tears. In the morning, he accepted *'Islām* and leaving behind the church and its wealth and material, he spent his life in the service of the *'Ahl al-Bayt*.

In the morning, the malicious people opened the pouch of *'ashrafis* to distribute them amongst themselves and all the *'ashrafis* had turned to that of dirt. On one side of them, it was written:

وَلَا تَحْسَبَنَّ اللّٰهَ غَافِلًا عَمَّا يَعْمَلُ الظّٰلِمُوْنَ

Certainly do not consider Allāh to be unaware of the doings of the oppressors.[66]

[65] *Sharḥ al-Ṣudūr, Bāb Ziyārah al-Qubūr wa `Ilm al-Mawtā, Pg. 212*

[66] *The Glorious Qur'ān, Sūrah 'Ibrāhīm: 42*

And on the other side, it was written:

وَسَيَعْلَمُ الَّذِينَ ظَلَمُوٓا أَيَّ مُنقَلَبٍ يَنقَلِبُونَ

And soon those who oppress shall learn what return they will be overturned.[67]

[67] *The Glorious Qur'ān, Sūrah al-Shu`arā': 227*

36

OTHER OCCURRENCES

When the blessed head of the Oppressed 'Imām, Allāh Almighty is pleased with him, reached the most tyrant oppressor, the filthy Yazīd, he began touching it with a reed. A delegate of the Christian king of Rome was present. He became astonished and said, "Back home, there is a hoof of the donkey of `Īsā, upon him be salutations, in a church of an island. Every year, we travel towards it like in *Ḥajj* from faraway places and we make solemn vows. We revere it just as you all honor your *Ka`bah,* and you have dealt with the son of your Prophet in this manner? I testify that you all are upon falsehood!"

A Jew said, "There is a gap of seventy generations between Dāwūd, upon him be salutations, and myself, yet the Jews honor me. You have killed the son of your own Prophet yourselves?"

Thereafter, this caravan was made to depart from Greater Syria (*Shām*) to *Madīnah Ṭayyibah*. The date of reaching *Madīnah* brought with itself the arrangements of Doomsday. There was chaos in every home. There flowed heart-wrenching and liver-wounding affliction from the doors and walls.

37

THE OCCURRENCES THAT FOLLOWED

After the martyrdom, blood poured from the sky. Naṣrah 'Azdīyah says, "When we awoke in the morning, we found all the dishes to be filled with blood. The sky became so dark that stars were seen in the daytime. In Greater Syria (*Shām*), whichever rocks would be lifted, fresh blood would be found beneath them."

In one narration, it says that for one week, the sky became so dark that the walls seemed to have been sheets painted by a deep red color. An upheaval could be witnessed amongst the stars, one star would crash against another.

'Abū Sa`īd says, "In the entire world, whichever rock was lifted, fresh blood was found beneath it. Blood poured from the sky. Clothing continued to tear, but its effects were not to leave, and nor did they. There was blood all over the homes and walls of Khorasan, Greater Syria (*Shām*), and *Kūfah*."

The scholars say, "This deep redness seen on the horizon was not there prior to the blessed martyrdom. The edges of the horizon remained red for six months and afterwards, this redness appeared."

38

THE FATE OF THE ILL-FATED INVOLVED IN THE MURDER OF THE ʿIMAM

ʿAbū al-Shaykh narrates, "Some people were sitting and discussing that anyone who aided in the murder of the Oppressed ʿImām, Allāh Almighty is pleased with him, surely became afflicted by some calamity or another. One old man said regarding his own impure self, 'Nothing happened to this man.' He stabilized the candle in the lantern and the fire caught onto this ill-fated individual. Yelling, 'Fire! Fire!' he dove into the Euphrates, but the fire was not extinguished, and he ended up in the [abode of] fire."

Manṣūr bin `Ammār narrates, "The murderers of the ʿImām suffered such thirst that they would down water pouches one after another, but the thirst would fail to decrease."

Sadamī says, "Someone hosted a gathering for me in *Karbalā*. The people discussed amongst themselves, 'Whoever participated in the murder of Ḥusayn, Allāh Almighty is pleased with him, died a horrible death.' The host belied him and said, 'That individual was also in that very army.' The next night, he rose to stabilize a lantern and the fire leaped and caught onto his body. By Allāh, I saw that his body had turned to coal!"

'Imām Zuhrī says, "Of them, some were killed, some had died after becoming blind, and some of their faces had blackened."

'Imām Wāqidī says, "One old man was present at the time of the 'Imām's martyrdom and did not become involved. He went blind."

When the reason was asked, he said, "He saw Muṣṭafā, may Allāh Almighty send blessings and salutations upon him and his progeny, in a dream with his sleeves rolled up holding an unsheathed sword in the sanctified hand. Ten murderers of Ḥusayn, Allāh Almighty is pleased with him, laid slaughtered. His Eminence, may Allāh Almighty send blessings and salutations upon him and his progeny, expressed wrath towards this old man and said, 'Whilst being present, you allowed this group to go forth?' He then applied to his eyes an applicator of the 'Imām's blood. When he awoke, he was blind."

Sibṭ 'ibn al-Jawzī narrates, "The individual who hung the blessed head of the Oppressed 'Imām from his horse, his face became darker than coal after a few days. The people said, 'Your face was fresh and mellow amongst all of Arabia, what predicament is this?' He responded, 'Ever since I lifted that head, every night, two individuals come, take me by the arm to a blazing fire, and push me in. My head bows and the fire strikes my face.' He then died in horrible conditions."

One old man saw His Luminous Eminence, may Allāh Almighty send blessings and salutations upon him and his progeny, in a dream and that before him there is blood in a basin. People are being presented to him, and His Eminence, may Allāh Almighty send blessings and salutations upon him and his progeny, blemishes them with that blood. When this man's turn came, he said, "I was not present."

He responded, "You did will it by heart." He then signaled towards him with the blessed finger, and he woke up blind in the morning.

Ḥākim narrates that Jibrīl said to His Luminous Eminence, may Allāh Almighty send blessings and salutations upon him and his progeny, "Allāh Almighty says, 'In return for Yaḥyā bin Zakarīyā, I killed seventy thousand, and in exchange for Ḥusayn, I will kill seventy thousand plus seventy thousand.'" [68]

Al-Ḥamdu li Allāh! Allāh, the Sublime and the Majestic, took the revenge of the 'Imām, Allāh Almighty is pleased with him, from the malicious 'Ibn Ziyād. When that outcast died, his head, alongside that of his companions, was brought and placed. There was a crowd of people and commotion was raised saying, "It has come! It has come!"

The narrator says, "I saw that a snake was coming. Going through all of the heads, it reached the impure head of 'Ibn Ziyād.

[68] *al-Mustadrak, Kitāb Tawārīkh al-Mutaqaddimīn, Qiṣṣah Qatl Yaḥyā, upon him be salutations, Ḥadīth: 4208, Vol. 3, Pg. 485*

It entered from one nostril, exited out the other nostril, and left. Commotion arose again saying, 'It has come! It has come!' That very snake had come back and did the same. A few times, the same happened."

Manṣūr says, "I saw an individual in Greater Syria (*Shām*) whose face was that of a swine. When I asked the reason, it was said, 'He used to curse Mawlā `Alī, may Allāh Almighty ennoble his noble countenance, and his pure progeny. One night, he saw His Eminence, the Master of the Universe, may Allāh Almighty send blessings and salutations upon him and his progeny, in a dream and 'Imām Ḥasan Mujtabā, Allāh Almighty is pleased with him, complained about this malicious individual. His Eminence, upon him be blessings and salutations, cursed him and spat on his face. His face turned to that of a swine.'"

والعياذ بالله رب العالمين

Refuge is with Allāh, the Lord of all Worlds!

تمّ بحمد الله

The End.

ABOUT THE AUTHOR

Muftī Sayyid `Abdul Ṣamad al-Qādirī is a *murīd* (spiritual disciple) of Sayyidī Tāj al-Sharī`ah Muftī 'Akhtar Riḍā Khān and a dedicated student of Muftī Faizān ul-Muṣṭafā al-Qādirī, the esteemed grandson of Ṣadr al-Sharī`ah. He graduated as a Muftī in Madīnah Munawwarah at the hands of his teacher in Ramaḍān 1444 AH. He has been granted *khilāfah* by the son of Tāj al-Sharī`ah, Qā'id al-Millah Muftī `Asjad Riḍā' Khān and many *'ijāzāt* by Muḥaddith Kabīr `Allāmah Ḍiyā' al-Muṣṭafā al-Qādirī. He is scholar trusted by the likes of Muftī Zāhid Ḥussain al-Qādirī and Muftī 'Afthāb Cāssim. Notably, Muftī `Abdul Ṣamad serves as the lead author and translator for TheSunniWay, a significant initiative led by Muftī Zāhid Ḥussain al-Qādirī, through which this book is presented. Currently, he resides in Silver Spring, Maryland, USA.

TheSunniWay

www.ingramcontent.com/pod-product-compliance
Lightning Source LLC
Chambersburg PA
CBHW021635120626
46545CB00002B/546
* 9 7 8 1 9 5 7 7 7 3 1 0 0 *